ACOUSTIC GUITAR
WEEKLY WORKOUTS

CHORDS AT YOUR FINGERTIPS

Guided by the master teachers who create *Acoustic Guitar* magazine's acclaimed Weekly Workouts, follow a series of step-by-step lessons to put chords, harmonies, and progressions at your fingertips

string
letter
media

Publisher: David A. Lusterman
Editor: Adam Perlmutter
Managing Editor: Kevin Owens
Music Proofreader: Mark Althans
Design and Production: Bill Evans
Production Manager: Hugh O'Connor

Cover Photograph: Bill Evans

ISBN 978-1-936604-37-1

This book was produced by String Letter Publishing, Inc.
941 Marina Way S., Suite E, Richmond, CA 94804
(510) 215-0010; stringletter.com

Contents

Video downloads to accompany each of the lessons and musical examples in this book are available for free at **store.acousticguitar.com/WWCAYF**. Just add the video tracks to your shopping cart and check out to get your free download.

Introduction

Weekly Workout has long been one of *Acoustic Guitar* magazine's most popular instructional formats. While the series is sometimes general in context and other times pegged to specific genres or applications, it always includes a series of progressively difficult exercises for both the hands and the mind. For this compilation of Weekly Workouts drawn from the magazine, the editors of *AG* have narrowed the focus to harmonic exercises. But within that theme, you'll find a range of different approaches that can help make you a stronger and deeper guitarist.

The book is organized into sections dealing with particular aspects of chord making. In the first portion, singer-songwriter and longtime *AG* editor at large Jeffrey Pepper Rodgers teaches how to bolster your rhythm work with handy, moveable shapes—grips that will provide a smart alternative to common barre chords, in any style. Berklee professor Jane Miller shows ways of using suspended chords to decorate your music, and jazz virtuoso and University of Colorado professor Sean McGowan demonstrates how to use drop-two chord voicings to strengthen both of your hands—not to mention your knowledge of the fretboard.

Next, Rodgers has a set of exercises based on the shuffling bass lines at the heart of many blues, rock, and R&B songs, as well as some workouts in which you'll stay on the low strings to build up some driving rock rhythms. Then, in a different approach to the low register, ace jazz guitarist and session musician Ron Jackson demonstrates first how to create walking bass lines and then ways of building chords on top of them—and playing those two separate components simultaneously.

The next section, on intervals, is a bit broader in scope. First, McGowan has you working out with major and minor thirds, in quite an athletic way, to imply a sense of harmonic motion. Adam Levy, the great guitarist, singer-songwriter, and sideman, teaches a similar concept, with decidedly different results, for you to exercise on using diatonic sixths in minor-key contexts.

In the next chapter, you'll further explore the interplay between harmony and melody as McGowan shows a way of deriving interesting voicings from different pentatonic scales—quite the workout, as the chords progress rapidly. Levy then teaches a less-is-more approach in which you'll learn smart ways of using horizontal lines to imply full chords.

Jackson wraps things up with a pair of demanding lessons—challenging in both their fingerboard calisthenics and the theory involved—in which you'll be reharmonizing basic chord voicings and will also learn to dress up melodies with chordal structures, one of the most demanding tasks for the fretting fingers.

As you progress through these lessons and begin to see the benefits to your guitar technique and your understanding of the fingerboard, remember not to lose sight of one thing: The ultimate goal of Weekly Workout—or any instruction in *AG*, for that matter—is to provide you with the tools for making music.

—Adam Perlmutter

Notation Guide

Reading music is no different than reading a book. In both cases, you need to understand the language that you're reading; you can't read Chinese characters if you don't understand them, and you can't read music if you don't understand the written symbols behind music notation.

Guitarists use several types of notation, including standard notation, tablature, and chord grids. Standard notation is the main notation system common to all instruments and styles in Western music. Knowing standard notation will allow you to share and play music with almost any other instrument. Tablature is a notation system exclusively for stringed instruments with frets—like guitar and mandolin—that shows you what strings and frets to play at any given moment. Chord grids use a graphic representation of the fretboard to show chord shapes for fretted stringed instruments. Here's a primer on how to read these types of notation.

Standard Notation

Standard notation is written on a five-line staff. Notes are written in alphabetical order from A to G. Every time you pass a G note, the sequence of notes repeats—starting with A.

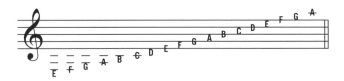

The duration of a note is determined by three things: the note head, stem, and flag. A whole note (○) equals four beats. A half note (♩) is half of that: two beats. A quarter note (♩) equals one beat, an eighth note (♪) equals half of one beat, and a 16th note (♬) is a quarter beat (there are four 16th notes per beat).

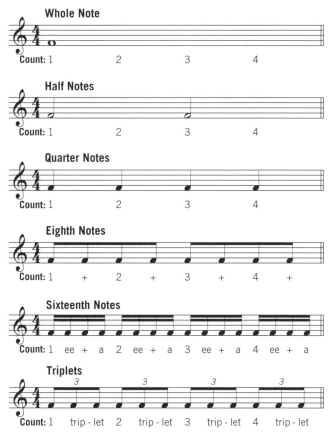

The fraction (4/4, 3/4, 6/8, etc.) or ¢ character shown at the beginning of a piece of music denotes the time signature. The top number tells you how many beats are in each measure, and the bottom number indicates the rhythmic value of each beat (4 equals a quarter note, 8 equals an eighth note, 16 equals a 16th note, and 2 equals a half note).

The most common time signature is 4/4, which signifies four quarter notes per measure and is sometimes designated with the symbol ¢ (for common time). The symbol ¢ stands for cut time (2/2). Most songs are either in 4/4 or 3/4.

Tablature

In tablature, the six horizontal lines represent the six strings of the guitar, with the first string on the top and sixth on the bottom. The numbers refer to fret numbers on a given string.

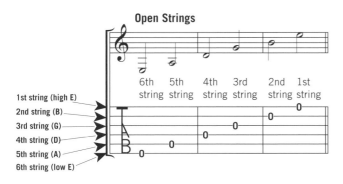

The notation and tablature in this book are designed to be used in tandem—refer to the notation to get the rhythmic information and note durations, and refer to the tablature to get the exact locations of the notes on the guitar fingerboard.

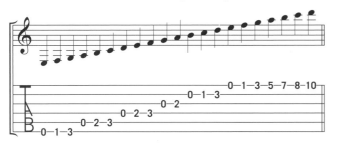

Fingerings

Fingerings are indicated with small numbers and letters in the notation. Fretting-hand fingering is indicated with 1 for the index finger, 2 the middle, 3 the ring, 4 the pinky, and *T* the thumb. Picking-hand fingering is indicated by *i* for the index finger, *m* the middle, *a* the ring, *c* the pinky, and *p* the thumb. Circled numbers indicate the string the note is played on. Remember that the fingerings indicated are only suggestions; if you find a different way that works better for you, use it.

Strumming and Picking

In music played with a flatpick, downstrokes (toward the floor) and upstrokes (toward the ceiling) are shown as follows. Slashes in the notation and tablature indicate a strum through the previously played chord.

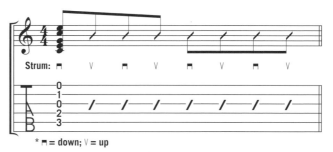

* ◼ = down; V = up

In music played with the pick-hand fingers, *split stems* are often used to highlight the division between thumb and fingers. With split stems, notes played by the thumb have stems pointing down, while notes played by the fingers have stems pointing up. If split stems are not used, pick-hand fingerings are usually present. Here is the same fingerpicking pattern shown with and without split stems.

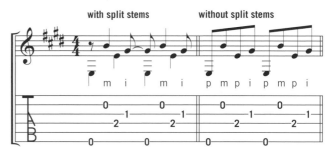

Chord Diagrams

Chord diagrams show where the fingers go on the fingerboard. Frets are shown horizontally. The thick top line represents the nut. A fret number to the right of a diagram indicates a chord played higher up the neck (in this case the top horizontal line is thin). Strings are shown as vertical lines. The line on the far left represents the sixth (lowest) string, and the line on the far right represents the first (highest) string. Dots show where the fingers go, and thick horizontal lines indicate barres. Numbers above the diagram are left-hand finger numbers, as used in standard notation.

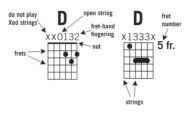

Again, the fingerings are only suggestions. An *X* indicates a string that should be muted or not played; 0 indicates an open string.

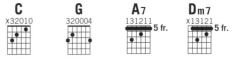

Capos

If a capo is used, a Roman numeral indicates the fret where the capo should be placed. The standard notation and tablature is written as if the capo were the nut of the guitar. For instance, a tune capoed anywhere up the neck and played using key-of-G chord shapes and fingerings will be written in the key of G. Likewise, open strings held down by the capo are written as open strings.

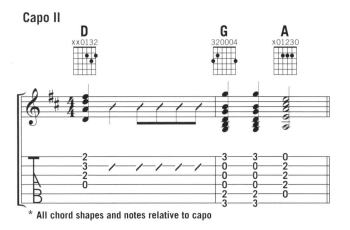

* All chord shapes and notes relative to capo

Tunings

Alternate guitar tunings are given from the lowest (sixth) string to the highest (first) string. For instance, D A D G B E indicates standard tuning with the bottom string dropped to D. Standard notation for songs in alternate tunings always reflects the actual pitches of the notes. Arrows underneath tuning notes indicate strings that are altered from standard tuning and whether they are tuned up or down.

Tuning: D A D G B E

Vocal Tunes

Vocal tunes are sometimes written with a fully tabbed-out introduction and a vocal melody with chord diagrams for the rest of the piece. The tab intro is usually your indication of which strum or fingerpicking pattern to use in the rest of the piece. The melody with lyrics underneath is the melody sung by the vocalist. Occasionally, smaller notes are written with the melody to indicate other instruments or the harmony part sung by another vocalist. These are not to be confused with cue notes, which are small notes that indicate melodies that vary when a section is repeated. Listen to a recording of the piece to get a feel for the guitar accompaniment and to hear the singing if you aren't skilled at reading vocal melodies.

Articulations

There are a number of ways you can articulate a note on the guitar. Notes connected with slurs (not to be confused with ties) in the tablature or standard notation are articulated with either a hammer-on, pull-off, or slide. Lower notes slurred to higher notes are played as hammer-ons; higher notes slurred to lower notes are played as pull-offs.

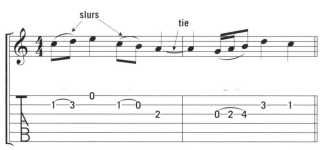

Slides are represented with a dash, and an S is included above the tab. A dash preceding a note represents a slide into the note from an indefinite point in the direction of the slide; a dash following a note indicates a slide off of the note to an indefinite point in the direction of the slide. For two slurred notes connected with a slide, you should pick the first note and then slide into the second.

Bends are represented with upward curves, as shown in the next example. Most bends have a specific destination pitch—the number above the bend symbol shows how much the bend raises the string's pitch: ¼ for a slight bend, ½ for a half step, 1 for a whole step.

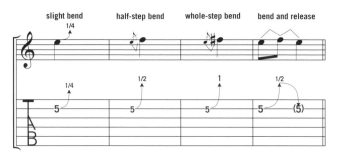

Grace notes are represented by small notes with a dash through the stem in standard notation and with small numbers in the tab. A grace note is a very quick ornament leading into a note, most commonly executed as a hammer-on, pull-off, or slide. In the first example below, pluck the note at the fifth fret on the beat, then quickly hammer onto the seventh fret. The second example is executed as a quick pull-off from the second fret to the open string. In the third example, both notes at the fifth fret are played simultaneously (even though it appears that the fifth fret, fourth string, is to be played by itself), then the seventh fret, fourth string, is quickly hammered.

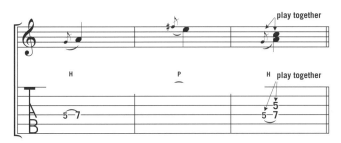

Harmonics

Harmonics are represented by diamond-shaped notes in the standard notation and a small dot next to the tablature numbers. Natural harmonics are indicated with the text "Harmonics" or "Harm." above the tablature. Harmonics articulated with the picking hand (often called artificial harmonics) include the text "R.H. Harmonics" or "R.H. Harm." above the tab. Picking-hand harmonics are executed by lightly touching the harmonic node (usually 12 frets above the open string or fretted note) with the right-hand index finger and plucking the string with the thumb or ring finger or pick. For extended phrases played with picking-hand harmonics, the fretted notes are shown in the tab along with instructions to touch the harmonics 12 frets above the notes.

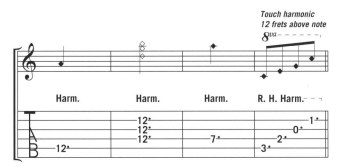

Repeats

One of the most confusing parts of a musical score can be the navigation symbols, such as repeats, *D.S. al Coda*, *D.C. al Fine*, *To Coda*, etc. Repeat symbols are placed at the beginning and end of the passage to be repeated.

You should ignore repeat symbols with the dots on the right side the first time you encounter them; when you come to a repeat symbol with dots on the left side, jump back to the previous repeat symbol facing the opposite direction (if there is no previous symbol, go to the beginning of the piece). The next time you come to the repeat symbol, ignore it and keep going unless it includes instructions such as "Repeat three times."

A section will often have a different ending after each repeat. The example below includes a first and a second ending. Play until you hit the repeat symbol, jump back to the previous repeat symbol and play until you reach the bracketed first ending, skip the measures under the bracket and jump immediately to the second ending, and then continue.

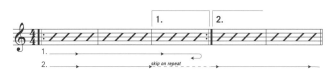

D.S. stands for *dal segno* or "from the sign." When you encounter this indication, jump immediately to the sign (𝄋). *D.S.* is usually accompanied by *al Fine* or *al Coda*. Fine indicates the end of a piece. A coda is a final passage near the end of a piece and is indicated with ⊕. *D.S. al Coda* simply tells you to jump back to the sign and continue on until you are instructed to jump to the coda, indicated with *To Coda* ⊕.

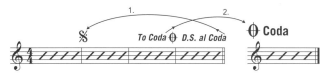

D.C. stands for *da capo* or "from the beginning." Jump to the top of the piece when you encounter this indication.

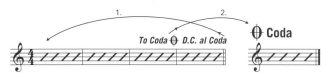

D.C. al Fine tells you to jump to the beginning of a tune and continue until you encounter the *Fine* indicating the end of the piece (ignore the *Fine* the first time through).

A Break from Barre-Hopping

Boost your rhythm playing with these movable, versatile chord shapes

By Jeffrey Pepper Rodgers

Barre chords are essential on the guitar, providing a set of shapes that you can move around the neck to form any chord. Yet they also can be—let's face it—a drag. They tire out your fretting hand when you need to hold them for long stretches, they can be cumbersome when you need to change chords quickly, and sometimes they just sound clunky. Fortunately, there are alternatives to barre chords that are also movable but are leaner, lighter sounding, and easier on the fingers. Those chords are the focus of this Weekly Workout.

The chord shapes in this lesson all use just three or four strings, with no open strings but no barres either. We will cover a range of chord types—major, minor, seventh, ninth, major seventh, sixth, and diminished—and put them to use in short progressions inspired by songs from the repertoires of the Allman Brothers, Eric Clapton, John Mayer, the Beatles, and more. These chords fit naturally in a blues or swing setting, but are also useful for creating punchy rhythm parts in any style of music and in any key.

WEEK ONE

First up is a set of movable major and minor chords. **Example 1** shows a series of voicings of G major and C minor; you can move these shapes up and down the neck to get other chords. For instance, move a G major shape up two frets to play A major, move it down two frets to play F major, and so on.

In all these chord diagrams, you'll see muted strings, marked with Xs. Use your fretting fingers for muting—just touch the unwanted strings lightly so they don't ring. For instance, in the first G shape in Ex. 1, lean your ring finger against the fourth string to mute it, and mute the top two

strings by resting your index finger on them (not pressing down). For the G/D in measure 1, mute the first string with the pad of your index finger, and also touch the sixth string with your ring finger. Muting the strings in this way allows you to strum all six strings—you'll hear the fretted notes along with a percussive scratch on the muted strings.

Not all of the chords in Ex. 1 have the root in the bass. Some have the fifth of the chord in the bass (G/D, Cm/G) or the third in the bass (G/B). These inversions can provide a nice change-up from standard root-based chord voicings, as you'll hear in the examples that follow.

In **Example 2**, try out some of these movable major or minor shapes in a short progression in the key of D. You can play this with a pick or fingerstyle—both work well (playing fingerstyle allows you to pick only the fretted strings, so you don't need to worry as much about muting). Throughout, the chord shapes are grouped in the same area on the neck to provide a smooth route through the progression; you start high on the neck, move down to the middle, and wind up around the third fret.

✔ *BEGINNERS' TIP #1*

Notice that many of these movable shapes are simplifications of barre chords you already know—with fewer strings and no barre.

WEEK TWO

This week, get bluesy by working with the seventh- and ninth-chord shapes shown in **Example 3**. The first G7 in measure 1 is a sweet-sounding voicing that requires much less muscle than a barre-chord G7 would; take out the B

WEEK 1

Example 1

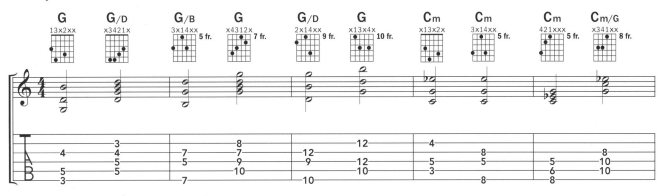

Example 2

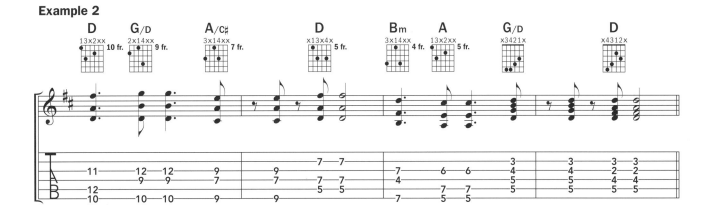

WEEK 2

Example 3

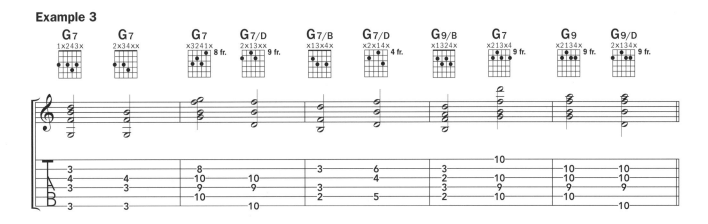

string to get the second G7 shape, which is even easier to fret and move around. That three-string G7 actually doesn't have all the notes of a G7—there is no D note. Other chords here are missing notes too—in fact, there is no G in the two G7/D shapes, the G7/B, the G9/B in measure 4, or the G9/D in measure 5. It might seem strange to call these G chords when they don't even have G's in them, but in context your ears fill in the root.

Now try out some of these new shapes in **Example 4**, based on T-Bone Walker's slow blues "Stormy Monday," as played by the Allman Brothers. The example is built around G7 and C7 chord shapes, with some embellishments: in measure 1, slide from the third to the fifth fret and back again on the B and D strings, then do the same thing in measure 2 on the C7

(this time sliding up and down on the high E and G strings). In the second half of measure 3, move the G7 shape up a fret for a G#7, then shift back down to G7 for measure 4.

Example 5 uses part of the progression from another classic blues song: "Nobody Knows You When You're Down and Out," written in the '20s by Jimmy Cox and famously covered by Eric Clapton. Notice how well these three-string chord shapes fit together as you move from C to E7/B to A7. Strum this in a percussive "choked" style, cutting off each chord quickly (shorter than the quarter-note duration shown) by loosening your fretting fingers right after you strum. Having this kind of easy control over how long notes ring is one of the big benefits of using chord forms with no open strings.

✔ *BEGINNERS' TIP #2*

For Ex. 4, count the 12/8 time in groups of three: 1 2 3, 2 2 3, 3 2 3, 4 2 3.

WEEK THREE

This week, work with one more set of movable shapes, for the jazzy major seventh, major ninth, sixth, minor seventh, and diminished chords. Play through the shapes in **Example 6**. With the Gmaj7 and Gmaj9 in measure 2, you can also move the bass note from the fifth string to the sixth at the same fret in order to put a D in the bass instead of the root. In measure 3, the second G6 is just a reduction of the first.

The last chord in this series, Cdim, may look familiar: it's the same shape used for the E7/B in Ex. 5, just one fret higher. In fact, this Cdim shape could be considered an F7/C. Similarly the G9/B shape in Ex. 4, measure 4, could also be called a Bm7♭5. (Jumping ahead in the lesson, you can see this shape in Ex. 10, measure 12, as a C♯m7♭5.) Sometimes the same chord shape can serve different purposes, and have different names, depending on the key of the song and the chord's function in the progression.

In **Example 7**, practice moving between a Gmaj7 and a C9/G; this is the main chord change in the off-the-beaten-track Pink Floyd tune "San Tropez." The pattern in **Example 8**, Gmaj7 to Dmaj7, is similar to what John Mayer uses in

WEEK 3

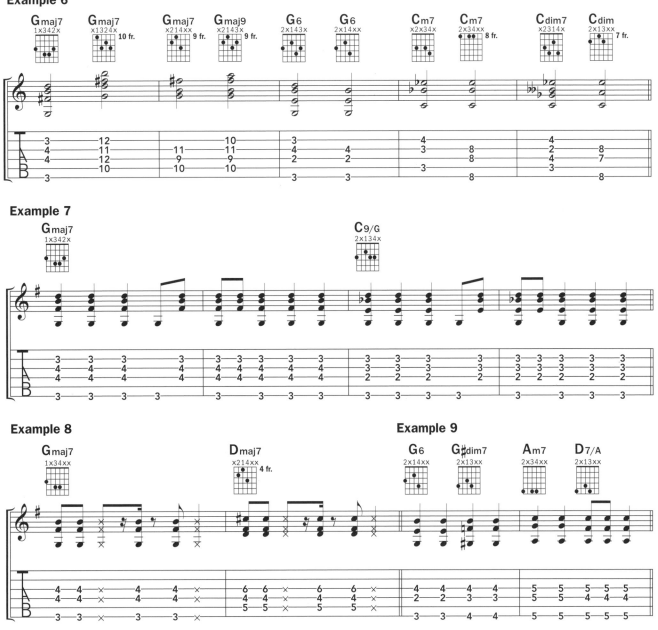

"Clarity"; play fingerstyle and for the backbeat percussion (marked with Xs in the notation) use your fretting hand to lightly slap the strings.

Finally, in **Example 9**, try out a classic swing-style turnaround that, in numbers terms, goes from I (in this case, G6) to #Idim (G#dim) to ii (Am7) to V (D7/A). Your fingers remain on the sixth, fourth, and third strings throughout and only move a couple of frets—it's a very efficient pattern.

✔ BEGINNERS' TIP #3

For additional practice with major seventh chords, check out '70s hits by America like "Tin Man," which mostly moves between Gmaj7 and Cmaj7.

WEEK FOUR

To wrap up this workout, play a longer progression that uses a variety of chord shapes covered in the previous weeks. The inspiration for **Example 10** is the Beatles' "Honey Pie," written by Paul McCartney as an homage to the vaudeville songs he and John Lennon loved growing up.

The example uses a lot of string percussion on the backbeats, in big-band swing style; the basic pattern is to strum on beats 1 and 3 and loosen your fretting hand to get snare-drum-like snaps on beats 2 and 4. In measures 7 and 8, play a turnaround similar to the one in Ex. 9, in this case going from I (G6 and then G/B) to ♭VI (E♭7/B♭) to V (D7/A). In measure 9, there's a long but quick slide up the neck to the F# at the ninth fret that launches into the second section of the song. In measure 18, jump back to the top for one last run through of the first section. Add a clarinet (or kazoo!) solo over these changes and you'll really have the sound dialed in.

As you are working on your own songs and arrangements, if you feel boxed in by barre chords, try substituting these movable shapes. Look for groups of chord voicings that are close together on the neck, so you can move easily from chord to chord, and try the progression in a few locations—below the fifth fret, around the middle of the neck, and up high. You are bound to discover some fresh sounds, and your fingers will no doubt appreciate the break from barre hopping.

✔ BEGINNERS' TIP #4

In Ex. 10, strum all the quarter notes with downstrokes. For the eighth notes (measures 8, 18, 19) use a down-up strum.

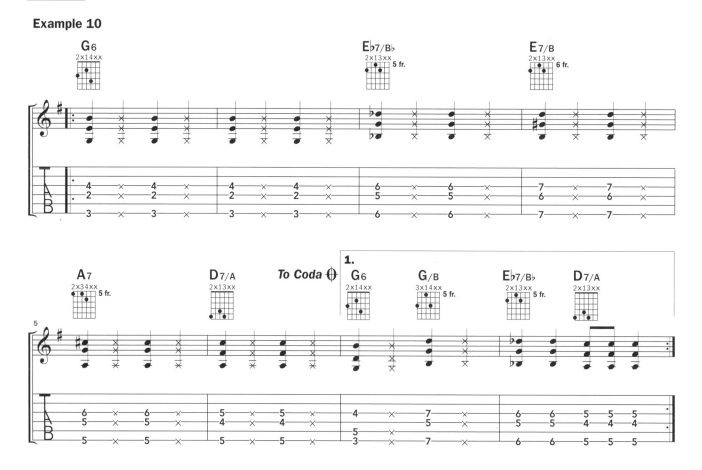

WEEK 4

Example 10

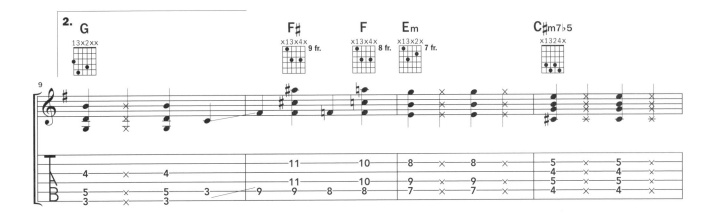

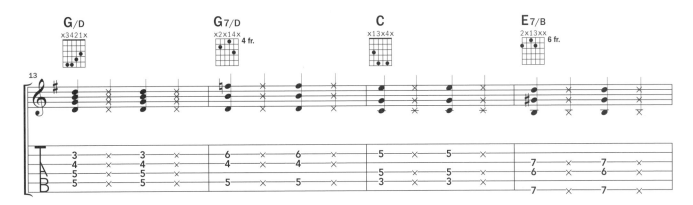

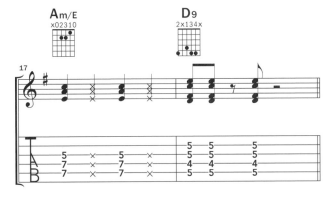

D.C. al Coda

Suspended in Harmony
How to harness the power of sus chords in your music

By Jane Miller

When you see the suffix -sus in a chord, as in Dsus4 or Dsus2, how do you know what to play? The sus is short for suspended and it's telling you to replace the third of a chord with the fourth or second. Since the third of a chord is the note that indicates major (natural third) or minor (flatted third), suspended chords have an ambiguous sound. This open-ended quality can lend interest and tension to music. Sus chords are also great—and diverse—tools for dressing up otherwise plain progressions.

In this lesson, you'll look at some sus chord symbols commonly seen in popular music and learn how to play them on guitar. But first, it's important to understand the construction of chords so that you are able to find the third and replace it with the indicated note. Major triads have three notes: the root, the third, and the fifth. Start with the name of the chord, such as D major, and call that root note 1 (D). Take the third and fifth notes of the major scale of the same name—in this case, D major (D E F# G A B C#)—and you have a D major triad: D (1) F# (3) A (5).

WEEK ONE

In a sus4, the most common type of suspended chord, the third is replaced with the fourth. So, take your D chord and swap out the third (F#) for the fourth note of the scale (G) and you have a Dsus4 (D G A). Try the most common Dsus4 chord, with the fourth as the highest note (**Example 1**).

In context, a suspended chord often resolves to the major triad with the same root note. This familiar sound, similar to what Carly Simon played in "Anticipation" or what's heard in Crosby, Stills, Nash & Young's "Carry On," is shown in **Example 2** with the progressions Dsus4–D and Asus4–A. To play the first two bars, start with a basic open-D chord grip and, keeping that shape depressed, add your fourth finger to the fourth-fret G. Then, to resolve to the D chord, lift your fourth finger from string 1, as the D chord's third is pre-fretted. Similarly, in bar 3, fret an open-A chord with your first, second, and third fingers, and grab the fourth (D) of the Asus4 chord (A D E) with your fourth finger, this time on string 2.

WEEK 1

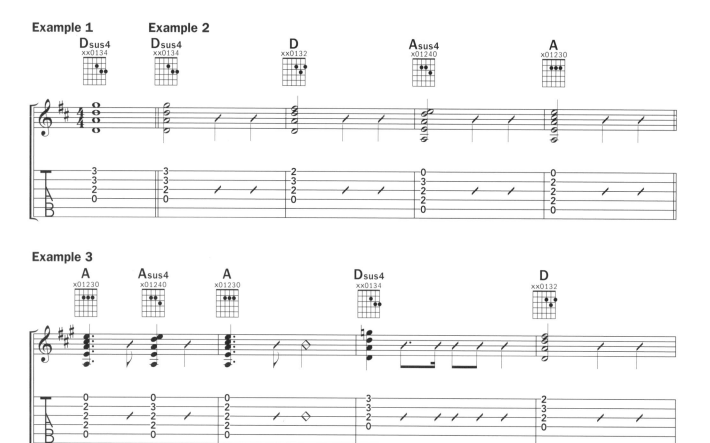

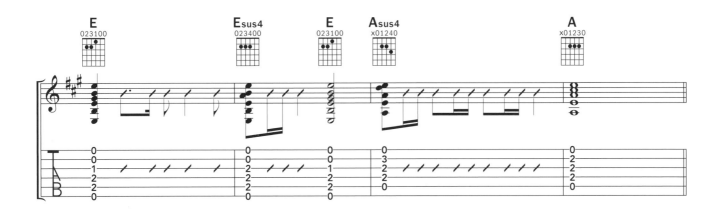

WEEK 2

Example 4   **Example 5**

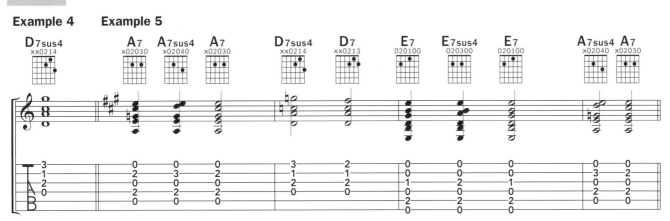

WEEK 3

Example 6   **Example 7**

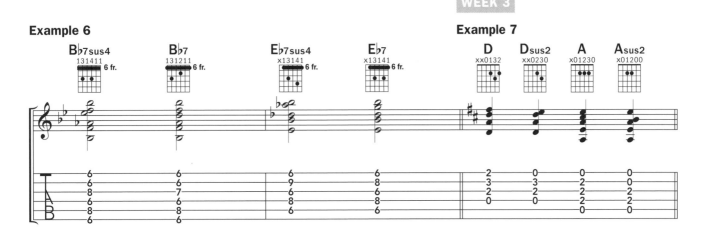

Example 8

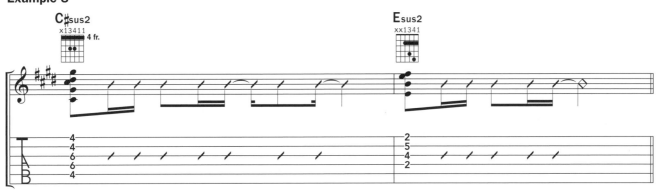

Example 3 runs through a common three-chord progression (I–IV–V) in the key of A major, with Esus4 joining the party. Use the same fingering trick as you did with the Dsus4 and Asus4 chords: fret the Esus4's fourth, A, with your fourth finger on string 3, then let go to the chord's third (G#).

✔ *Beginners' Tip #1*
A good way to learn new chords from ones you already know is to write out note names across the top of a chord diagram, like D A D F# for an open D chord. Then, at the bottom of the diagram, label the function of each note, such as 1 5 1 3. That way, you can easily locate the third and replace it with a suspension.

WEEK TWO
Suspended chords can also be made from dominant sevenths—a sound heard in jazz compositions like Herbie Hancock's "Maiden Voyage." Take your D triad, for instance, add the flatted seventh degree (C) of the D major scale, and you've got a D dominant seventh chord (D F# A C), labeled simply as D7. With the same method you used for creating sus4 triads, you can construct a D7sus4 chord (D G A C)—try the typical guitar fingering shown in **Example 4**. A reworking of Ex. 3 will give you the progression found in **Example 5**, using 7sus4s that resolve to dominant seventh chords.

Pay special attention to the E and A chord forms in these examples. All of these fingerings will work with barre chords, making them moveable and easy to transpose to any root. **Example 6** uses the E forms for a B♭7sus4-to-B♭7 move and the A forms for an E♭7sus4–E♭7 progression, all with a sixth-fret barre.

✔ *Beginners' Tip #2*
Give yourself extra time to learn barre chords if they're new to you. The sweet spot for any fretted note is close behind the fret; aim for getting your first finger straight across all six strings in this location. For even pressure, practice rolling your first finger back so that you're using the side of the finger that is closest to your thumb.

WEEK THREE
You might recognize another suspended chord type—sus2—from popular music. The Police's "Message in a Bottle" is but one of many good examples of this chord in action. And you might already be using a sus2 when you add decorative hammer-ons and pull-offs to a D or A chord.

Just as in a sus4 chord, a sus2 replaces the third—this time, as the name indicates, with the second. Play a D major triad and let go of your second finger, and you'll have a

WEEK 4

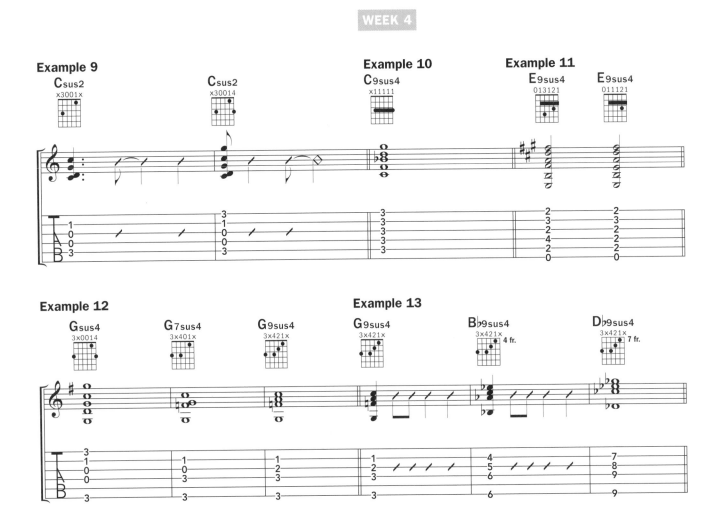

Dsus2 chord (**Example 7**). The note that you've taken away is F♯; the note that you've replaced it with is E, or the open first string. It works just as easily for the A major chord when you lift your third finger, leaving the B string (the chord's second) open and taking away the C♯ (third). (Note that this is different from an add9 chord, which contains both the ninth/second and the third.)

Move the Asus2 form around the neck freely using a barre and finding the root on the fifth string. Need a C♯sus2 chord? No problem—use a fourth-fret barre, as shown in **Example 8**. The Dsus2 form can be moved around as well, by making a half-barre with the root of the chord on the fourth string. Play it with your first finger at fret 2, and you've got the Esus2 shown in bar 2.

A Csus2 chord (**Example 9**) can be thought of as a basic open-C shape with the second finger omitted and the chord's second (D) played on the open fourth string. To avoid accidentally hitting the open first string (E), you can double the open G at the octave on string 1 with your fourth finger, as in bar 2.

✔ *Beginners' Tip #3*
A good rule of thumb for the sus2 barre chords shown—and for most chords, in fact—is this: skip a fret, skip a finger. So, skip your second finger and use your third and fourth fingers
to play the chord forms when they begin two frets above the first-finger barre.

WEEK FOUR

For extra color, try adding a ninth to any 7sus4 chord. For instance, barre the third fret with your first finger across strings 5–1 to get the C9sus4 (**Example 10**). This particular voicing, spelled lowest note to highest, is C (1) F (4) B♭ (7) D (9). If you'd like, omit the chord's fifth, the third-fret G, as this note is inessential to the sonority.

Make an E9sus4 chord by playing a standard Bm7 barre chord at fret 2 and adding the low open E as the bass note. Notice that the ninth, F♯, does double duty on strings 4 and 1. If you'd prefer to double the root (E) instead, lift your third finger to reveal the E on string 4, fret 2. **Example 11** shows both options.

A Gsus4 chord presents a problem that can be solved by blocking the fifth string, as notated in **Example 12**. If you want to play a G7sus4, fret the flatted seventh (F) on string 4 with your fourth finger and block the first string. One more step makes a jazzy-sounding G9sus4; just add your second finger to string 3, fret 2, giving you the ninth (A).

If you isolate the upper three notes of that G9sus4 chord, you'll discover an F major triad (F A C). So G9sus4 could also

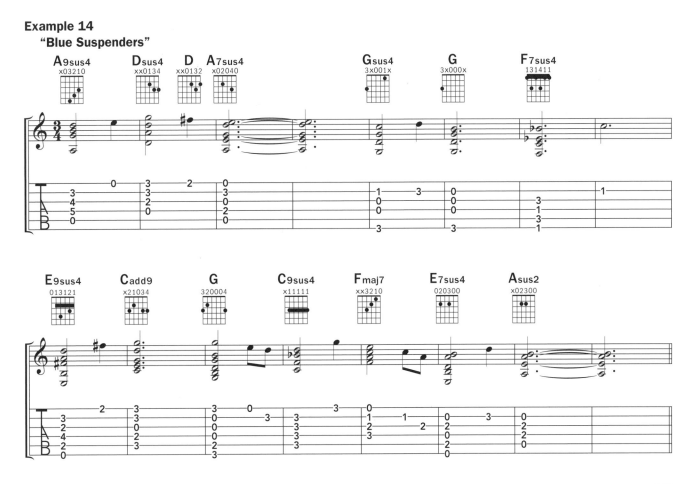

Example 14
"Blue Suspenders"

be called F/G—an F triad with G in the bass. This formula gives you another moveable shape: any major triad played with a bass note that is a whole step higher than the root of the triad creates a 9sus4 chord.

To play **Example 13**, keep the same fingering and move the G9sus4 up to fourth position to make a Bb9sus4 (Ab/Bb) chord, then to seventh position for Db9sus4 (Cb/Db). Carefully block strings 5 and 1 and listen to the wide-open sound of these chords; there's no need to resolve them.

Finally, use your ears and taste to incorporate some suspended chords into your own playing, songwriting, and arranging for guitar. In **Example 14**, you'll find a short piece, "Blue Suspenders," which demonstrates how you might integrate these harmonies with other chord types. As you get to know these fingerings, your ears will become accustomed to the sound of suspended chords and you'll find yourself working them into your playing naturally.

✔ *Beginners' Tip #4*

You can get up and running pretty quickly with A9sus4 and D9sus4 chords by taking advantage of open strings that fit these chords. When you play the open strings 5–1—A, D, G, B, and E—you've got an A9sus4 chord. When you add the C on string 2, fret 1, and strum strings 4–1, you get D G C E, which is D9sus4 without the fifth (A).

TAKE IT TO THE NEXT LEVEL

Once you've completed this lesson, try resolving 9sus4 chords, just like you did with triads. You might take it even further and flatten the ninth, creating a more urgent need for resolution. For example, play A9sus4, turn it into A7b9, and resolve it to either a D major- or D minor-type chord. The voicings in this example are all moveable and therefore easily transposed. Call any dominant chord V and count down to I to land on the home chord.

Take It to the Next Level

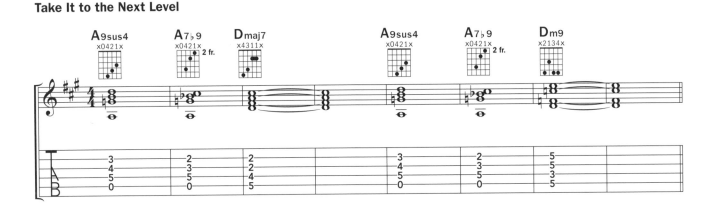

A suspended and extended chord like this A9sus4 grip can add sophistication to your music.

Drop-Two Chord Changes

Strengthen your picking and fretting hands with these popular four-note chord voicings

By Sean McGowan

Drop-two chord voicings are popular with guitarists of all styles, owing to their ease of fingering, reasonable three-to-four-fret span, and pleasing sound. The term drop two comes from big band jazz and orchestral arrangers who, when creating parts for four horns or stringed instruments, would number them one to four (typically the highest to lowest notes in a chord voicing). This is comparable to SATB (soprano, alto, tenor, bass) parts in a four-part vocal choir—you can think of the second part as the alto part. One way arrangers would create interesting textures would be to simply lower, or drop, one of the parts in a standard chord voicing down an octave. Drop two literally means that the second part is dropped an octave. For example, a Cmaj7 voicing C–E–G–B (low to high) becomes G–C–E–B when the G is dropped an octave to create a drop-two voicing.

In this series of workouts we'll explore drop-two chord arpeggios, working through a variety of chord types using diatonic chords of major and melodic minor scales, all the while

getting a comprehensive workout for the fretting and picking hands. These exercises may be practiced with a pick or played fingerstyle, and you should pay close attention to the suggested fingerings and articulations.

The reward in these exercises comes from the finger-switching combinations that occur as you change voicings, and the string crossings required by the picking hand. Unless notated otherwise, use strict alternate picking for each example, and be sure to work with a metronome, starting at a slow tempo. Strive for good tone and accuracy instead of speed, which will come naturally after playing these slowly and faithfully over the course of a month.

WEEK ONE

The first week's workout introduces five basic drop-two chord types and shapes, all played with the root on the fifth string. We'll take each chord shape and move it up and down the

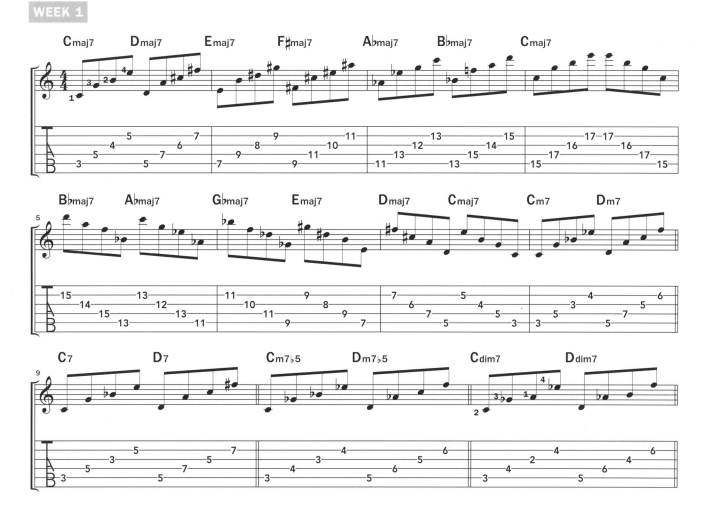

neck in whole steps. Measure 1 starts with a Cmaj7 chord, followed by Dmaj7, Emaj7, etc. all the way up to the 15th-position Cmaj7. If you don't have a cutaway, the arpeggios in measure 4 may be difficult to reach, but you can still get a good workout if you omit this measure and go straight from measure 3 to measure 5. Play the individual notes of each chord from low to high using alternate picking for each note. This exercise involves a lot of string crossing and will warm up your picking hand much more efficiently than playing scales. Play through the examples slowly at first, and try to avoid excessive tension in your picking hand: don't squeeze your pick too hard. If you are playing fingerstyle, play each ascending chord with a *p–i–m–a* pattern or practice alternating strokes with *i–m* ascending and descending.

The other four chord types are minor seventh (measure 8), dominant seventh (measure 9), m7♭5 or half diminished (measure 10), and diminished seventh (measure 11). These root-position forms are all movable and have unique fingerings to give your fretting hand a solid workout. For each chord, I've notated just the first two voicings, but be sure to move them all the way up and then back down the neck as with the major seven voicings in measures 1–7.

WEEK TWO

In Week Two's workout, we'll use the various chord types from the first week to play through the diatonic chords of a C major scale. Diatonic seventh chords are simply four-part seventh chords in a major (or minor) key that are built by stacking the notes of the scale in intervals of thirds. So the first diatonic chord of C major (C–D–E–F–G–A–B) would be Cmaj7 (C–E–G–B), the second chord is Dm7 (D–F–A–C), and so on.

We'll keep the roots of the chords on the fifth string, but change the patterns to take the workout up a notch for the picking hand. This week's exercise will also be a little more challenging for your fretting hand than the first week's, because the fingerings change every two beats as you move through the different chord types. Be sure to use the same fingerings for each type of chord you used in week one. Again, if you don't have a cutaway, measures 4 and 5 will be a stretch. You can either skip those measures or use the alternate fingerings for the Bm7♭5 and Cmaj7 chords shown in measure 9, which move the drop-two chords up onto the top four strings (we'll get to complete drop-two voicings on the top strings in Week Three).

WEEK THREE

This week's workout involves a technique often used in jazz and country guitar styles called hybrid picking, in which you use a pick (held between the thumb and index finger) in conjunction with the middle, ring, and little fingers of your picking hand to pluck or arpeggiate a chord. For the ascending patterns here, play the lowest note of each chord with the pick and use your middle, ring, and little fingers to play the remaining three notes (low to high) of each arpeggio. The descending pattern is slightly different, with your ring finger picking the top note, followed by the pick on the fourth string, and the middle and ring fingers plucking the two notes on the third and second strings. You could use your little finger for the top note, but you'll probably find that your ring finger is stronger and produces a better tone. You can also play this fingerstyle, using a *p–i–m–a* pattern on the fourth through first strings. Also, this week we are transferring our drop-two voicings to the top four strings in the key of F major, resulting

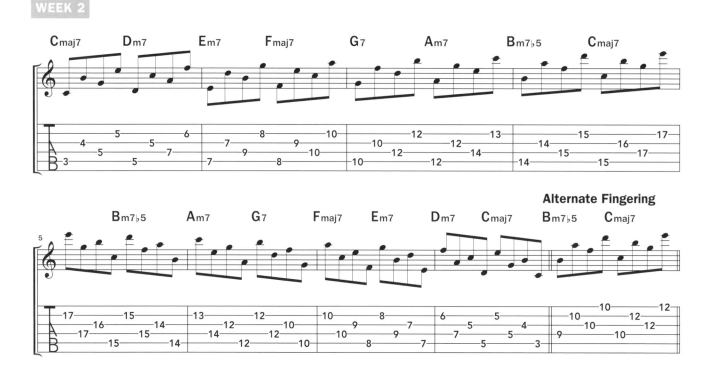

in slightly different shapes and fingerings for each chord. Even though we are in a different key, you'll notice that the sequence of diatonic chord types is the same.

WEEK FOUR

Now we'll move the diatonic seventh chords back to the middle string set, this time in the key of B♭ major. We'll also increase the difficulty from previous weeks by playing each chord type in triplets. Be sure to work with a metronome to ensure the consistency

of your triplet rhythms. You may want to start by playing triplets on the open G string to hear and feel the rhythm before diving into the string-crossing patterns. Let's start in first position and move up the fingerboard in the key of B♭. Once we reach our home base (the tonic B♭ in 13th position), let's modulate down a half step to the key of A major and work our way down the neck. If you have the time and energy, you can continue this workout by moving back up the neck in C major and down in B, gradually moving through all the keys (or at least a few).

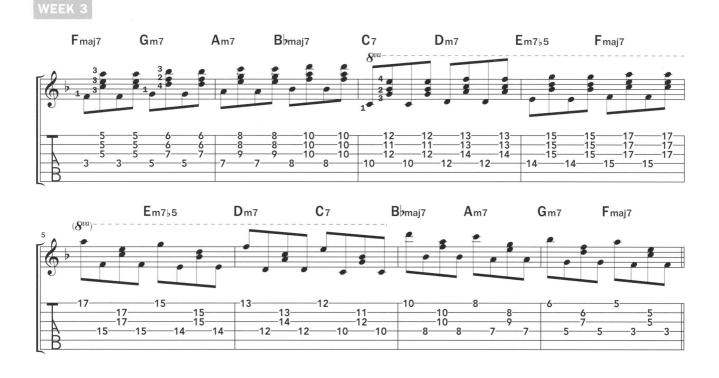

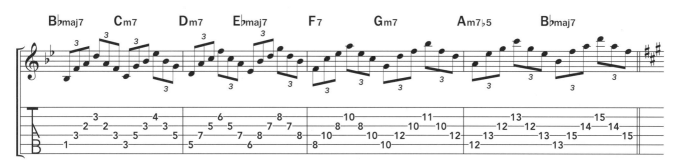

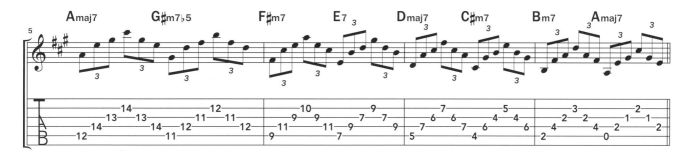

EXTRA CREDIT

For the first extra credit workout (**Example 1**), we'll explore some less common drop-two chord types. These each have unique sounds and character as well as unique fingerings for the fretting hand. **Example 2** puts some of these new chord types to use by working through a new set of diatonic chords of the C melodic minor scale. The melodic minor scale is just like the major scale, but with a lowered third scale degree, creating a minor tonality with strikingly beautiful chord types often used in jazz, pop, and classical chord progressions (such as Gershwin's "Summertime"). This example also mixes up the string sets by putting the first four chords on the middle strings and the second four on the top strings. Finally, **Example 3** uses directional picking (also called sweep picking) to play the diatonic seventh chords of F major on the top four strings. Directional picking moves through two or more notes on adjacent strings in one direction, using all down- or upstrokes depending on the direction of the musical line. This example starts with four notes crossing the top four strings, followed by a quarter note (the ninth of each chord) on the top string. If you're using a pick, use consecutive downstrokes for the four 16th notes, followed by an upstroke for the quarter note. If you're playing fingerstyle, roll through each 16th note rapidly, using a *p–i–m–a* pattern, followed by *i* for the quarter note. For the descending sequence, use up-strokes for the 16th notes, followed by a downstroke for the quarter note on the fourth string (also the ninth of the chord). Fingerstyle players should use *a–m–i–p* for the 16th notes, followed by *i* or *m* for the quarter note. These directional exercises are particularly challenging, so remember to take it slowly and solidly for best results.

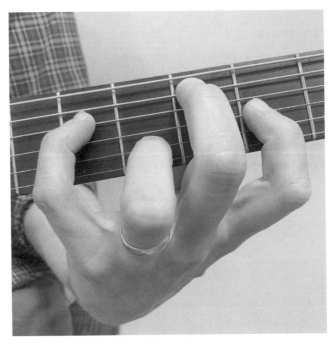

This Cm6 grip is a fine example of a less common drop-two chord with a striking sound.

Extra Credit

Example 1

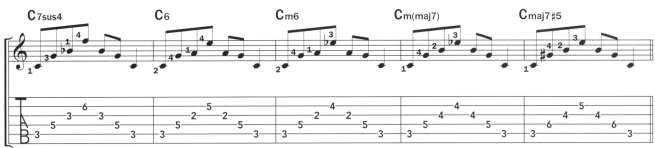

Example 2

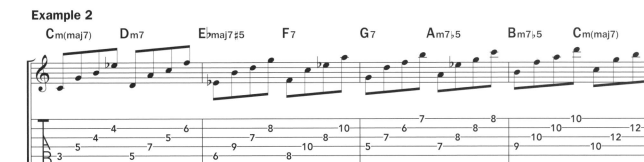

Example 3

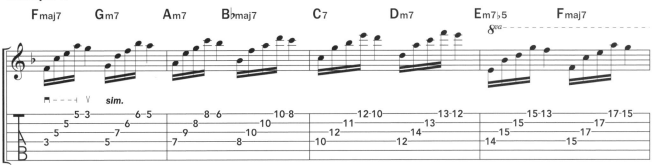

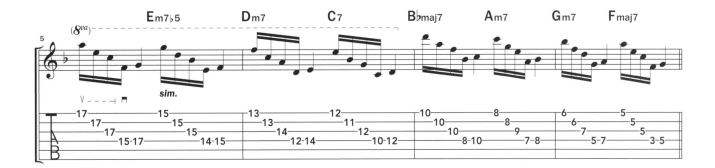

How Low Can You Go?

Playing around with blues bass lines

By Jeffrey Pepper Rodgers

Nothing does more to enhance a song's groove than a great bass line—and you don't need an actual bass to play one. The low end of the guitar can serve the same role as a bass, keeping the rhythmic pulse while moving the progression from chord to chord. For guitarists of any stripe, it's a very productive exercise to drop the chords and lead licks and focus on developing bass lines.

In this Weekly Workout, you will work with the perennial favorite song/jam form among guitarists: the 12-bar slow blues, as in "Goin' Down Slow" or "Stormy Monday," in the particularly guitar-friendly key of E. The ground rules are to use only single notes, and only the bottom three strings of the guitar, while still trying to create a full sound that could stand on its own.

WEEK ONE

The agenda this week is to establish a basic version of a slow blues in E, using only a bass line. After a bit of experimentation, the approach I arrived at was to deconstruct the typical blues-shuffle chord pattern—where on an E chord, for instance, you'd play a double stop on the open sixth string with the fifth string alternating between the second and fourth frets, and so on.

Here, rather than using double stops or full chords, play the root bass note (in measure 1, an E on the sixth string), quickly slide your ring finger from the second to the fourth fret on the fifth string, and then land on the second fret of the fifth string with your index finger. Follow the same pattern on the A and B chords, using a quick slide (shown with a grace note) to suggest the shuffle riff.

At the end of each measure, use another grace-note slide: on the E chord, up to a G♯; on the A chord, up to C♯; and on the B chord, up to D♯. These notes are all the major thirds of the underlying chords, so playing them creates a major-key sound. Though you're not playing any chords per se, the bass line is hitting the chord tones (root, third, fifth) and so establishing the harmony by itself. The last measure of the example finally breaks the grace-note slide pattern with a simple repetition of the B bass note in a triplet rhythm—setting you up to loop back around to the top (12 bars are never enough).

✔ *BEGINNERS' TIP #1*

The time signature 12/8 is often used for slow blues with a shuffle feel. Count it in four groups of three: 1 and a, 2 and a, 3 and a, 4 and a.

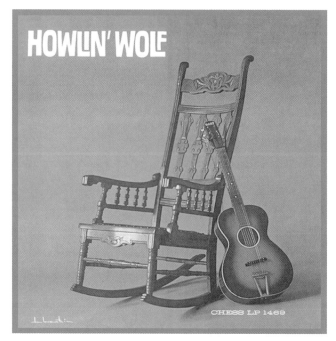

The bluesman Howlin' Wolf was a master of the sorts of bass-line moves featured in this lesson.

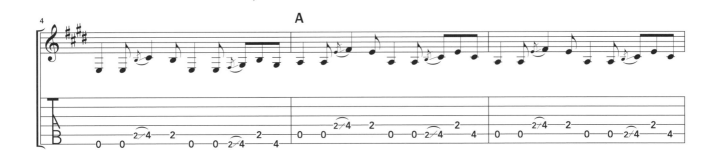

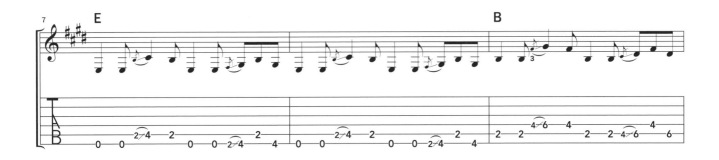

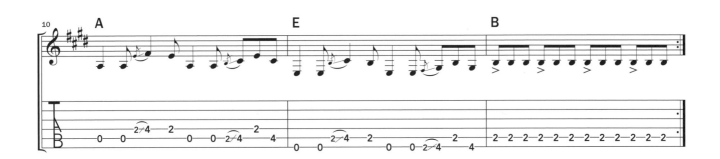

WEEK TWO

The Week One example accomplished the goal of conveying the 12-bar blues form using only a bass line, and now it's time to start making some variations. This week's idea is to underscore the chord changes by playing walk-ups to the root of each new chord.

The first walk-up comes at the end of measure 1, where you play F#, G, and G# on the sixth string on the way to the A at the beginning of measure 2. You're simply walking chromatically (a half step at a time) up to the root of the next chord. Do the same thing throughout the example, with either a three-note or two-note walk-up to each new root/chord. The one exception is the end of measure 9, where you walk *down* chromatically on the chord change from B to A.

The last two bars, the turnaround, carry the walk-up idea further. The bass line walks up to the B chord (G#, A, A#, B), hitting each note three times and alternating the higher octave (played on the fourth string) for added effect. Bass players use octaves like this all the time—and they work great on guitar, too.

✔ BEGINNERS' TIP #2

Try using palm muting for these bass lines. Rest the side of your picking-hand palm on the strings close to the saddle for a thumpy sound.

WEEK 2

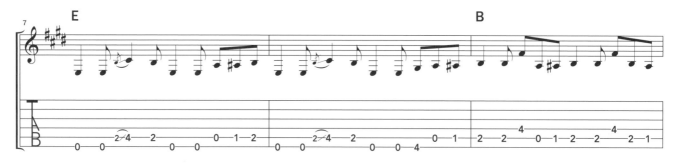

WEEK THREE

So far, as noted above, the bass lines have given this blues a major-key sound, by including the major thirds of the chords. This week, explore a darker shade of blue, by accentuating the blue notes—especially the flatted seventh and the flatted third. In the key of E, those blue notes are D♮ (flatted seventh) and G♮ (flatted third), and they pop up throughout the example. The chords are now written as E7, A7, and B7, and though the key signature is still E major, the flatted thirds in the bass line are bringing in a minor sound. That tension between major and minor is fundamental to blues.

As in previous weeks, this example uses a recurring pattern: an ascending line from the root to the sixth to the flat-ted seventh. On the E chord, that's E, C♯, D♮ (as in the beginning of measures 1, 4, and 8); and on the A chord, it's A, F♯, G♮ (measures 2, 5, and 6). There's also a repeating pull-off from the third fret to the open sixth string (measures 1, 4, and 5), plus an eighth-note run on the E (measure 3, 7, and 11). Repetitions like these help the bass line hang together, so the whole thing sounds like a song rather than a string of unrelated ideas.

✔ BEGINNERS' TIP #3

In this style, play the bass notes staccato: rather than letting notes ring, cut their durations short by muting with your fretting fingers.

WEEK 3

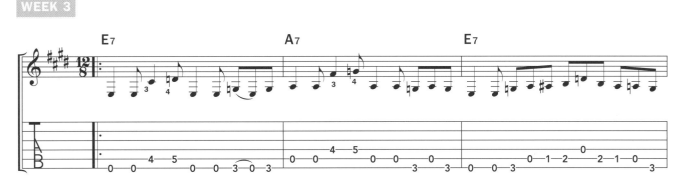

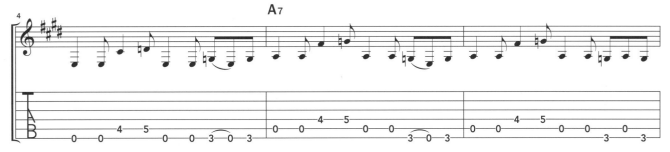

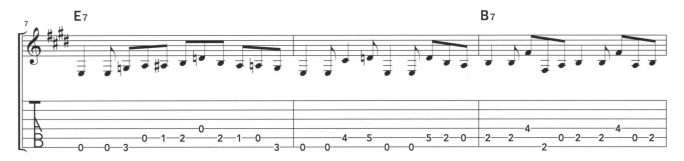

WEEK FOUR

A big reason guitarists love playing in E is, of course, the availability of open-string bass notes for E and A. Playing bass lines, you can take advantage of those open strings to travel up the neck. On a blues in E, there's an especially sweet zone between the fifth and seventh frets on the low strings, and that's the focus of this week's example.

Note that this bass line uses a grace-note slide similar to the one in Week One, except further up the neck. On the E7 chord, slide to a B note at the seventh fret of the sixth string, and on the A7, slide to an E note at the seventh fret of the fifth string. In the second half of measure 10, play the grace-note figures with hammer-ons rather than slides.

As in Week Three, this example uses a lot of blue notes for a darker feel. The bass line also takes advantages of the octaves available in this position: the E at the seventh fret of the fifth string

(an octave above the open sixth string) and the A at the seventh fret of the fourth string (an octave above the open fifth string). Closing out the example is a dramatic turnaround that descends for two measures, alternating notes on the fifth and fourth strings.

Now that you're in the groove of this E blues, try improvising your own variations, sticking to the rule of all single notes, only on the bottom three strings. You're bound to discover bass line ideas that you can incorporate into accompaniment as a break from full chords, or use for low-register riffs or solos. You can even be a faux bass player at a jam session with a bunch of guitars—your fellow jammers will thank you for it.

✔ *BEGINNERS' TIP #4*

Throughout the Week Four example, stay in fifth position, with your index finger at the fifth fret. Use your ring finger for notes at the seventh fret.

All About that Bass
How to play driving rock rhythm on the low strings

By Jeffrey Pepper Rodgers

When you want to rock out on rhythm guitar, it's a natural instinct to use big chords and big strums and play hard. But as with so many other aspects of the guitar (and music in general), more is not necessarily more. Often you can create more rhythmic drive and intensity by playing less. Think of songs with a classic, steady rock feel, like U2's "With or Without You," Radiohead's "Creep," and Creedence Clearwater Revival's "Fortunate Son"—the groove is all about the insistent pulse and the snap on the backbeats. If you want to create that kind of feel with one guitar, the best strategy is to lay off the heavy strumming, strip down the chords, and zero in on the low end and the beat.

That's why this lesson is all about that bass—no treble—and working the low strings to create stronger rock rhythms. Note that the focus here is *not* on developing single-note bass lines, but on playing chord patterns in the lower register of the guitar.

WEEK ONE

The first item on the agenda is to build a vocabulary of chord voicings on the low strings. You will recognize some of these as simply the bottom portion of full chord fingerings you already know, while others may be unfamiliar.

The chords in the first line of notation all use open strings. The first G is just the low end of a regular G major chord,

while the starker-sounding G5 has a unison D note on the fifth and fourth strings. You'll see that several of these chords are inversions, meaning that a note other than the root is in the bass: the A5/E has the fifth of the chord on the bottom, and the D/F♯ chords have the third on the bottom. Some chords shown here use just two strings (and any of the three-string chords could be stripped down to two for a leaner sound). For the E5 chord in measure 5, move up the neck while taking advantage of the bass note on the open sixth string.

The chords in the second line use no open strings, so are completely movable. You could, for instance, move the A fingering up two frets to play a B chord, then up one more fret to play a C, etc.

Get comfortable with these bassy chord voicings and try subbing them into songs you already play. You can use the 5 chords (G5, A5, etc.), which have no third that defines them as major or minor, in place of both major and minor chords in a progression. These are power chords—the building blocks of rock 'n' roll.

✔ *BEGINNERS' TIP #1*

The chords shown can be fingered in multiple ways. Try to use whatever fingering makes a song's chord changes the most economical.

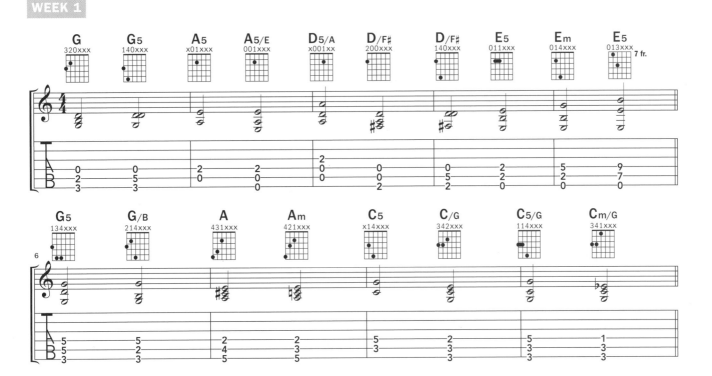

WEEK TWO

This week's exercise is based on the progression G–D–Em–C. In number terms that's I–V–vi–IV, as used in U2's "With or Without You" (in the key of D), Brandi Carlile's "The Story" (in A), and many other songs (check out Axis of Awesome's "4 Chords" on YouTube for a cheeky mashup of hits that use I–V–vi–IV). You could easily strum this progression using standard open-position chords, but try it as shown here, with three variations that use the low chord voicings introduced in Week One. The whole example has an unrelenting eighth note pulse. Rest the side of your pick-hand palm on the strings near the bridge to make the sound a little more thumpy, and play everything with downstrokes of the pick.

In the first variation (measures 1–4), the G, D/F♯, and E5 voicings create a nice descending bass line on the sixth string. Your fingers move very little from chord to chord—it's very economical. Notice the three-string chords that come up three times in each measure, following a pattern of 1 2 3, 1 2 3, 1 2. Try accenting these chords to give the rhythm a little extra drive. The second variation (measures 5–8) has the same bass motion

but a somewhat starker sound. Keep your pinky in place as you change from the G to the D/F♯, and again from Em to C5/G.

The third variation (measures 9–12) uses all closed-position fingerings, which can be great for rock rhythm because they're so easy to play percussively. This time, the bass notes of the chords go up the sixth string—from G to A, B, and C.

✔ *BEGINNERS' TIP #2*

Since you're only playing the bottom strings, use a very contained motion with your pick while keeping your palm on the bridge.

WEEK THREE

This week, muting and percussion are the focus, with an example based on the changes from Creedence's "Fortunate Son." This time-less rocker is power chords all the way, so you won't find any majors or minors here. Although "Fortunate Son" is in the key of G, the example is written in A. This is actually true to the way John Fogerty plays the song; he tunes down a whole step (to D), so his key-of-A fingerings sound in the key of G.

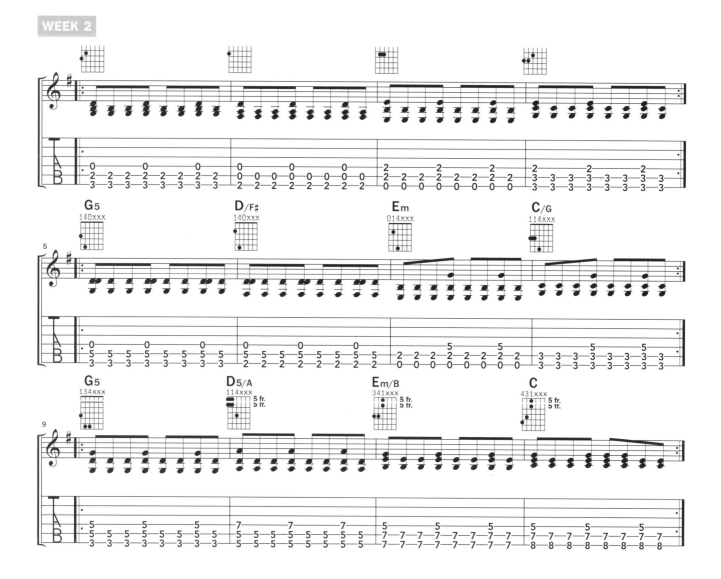

WEEK 3

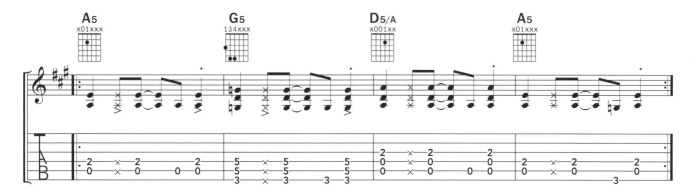

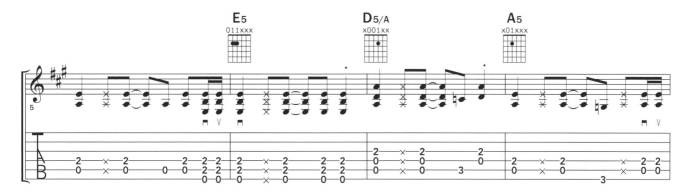

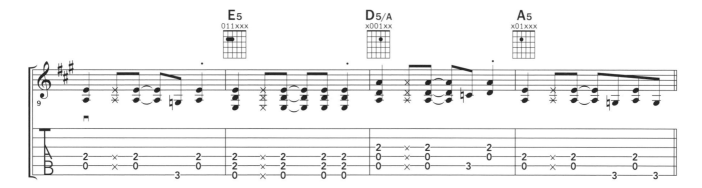

The chord fingerings are the same as used earlier in this lesson, except the E5 is played with an index-finger barre. Work on bringing out the backbeats—beats 2 and 4 (marked with accents in the first couple of measures). On beat 2 of every measure, play a percussive scratch—loosen your fretting fingers on whatever chord you're holding, lay them across the strings without pressing down, and give the muted bass strings a whack with the pick. On beat four of many measures, you'll see a staccato dot. This means play the chord shorter than written (if it's a quarter note, play it more like an eighth) by muting with your fretting fingers. To stop open strings from ringing, lay your fretting fingers across them, too.

At the end of measures 5 and 8, play a quick 16th-note strum (think Pete Townshend) to propel into the next measure. And in several spots, add a little bass riff: in measures 4, 8, 9, and 12, reach for a G on the sixth string under an A5 chord; and in measures 7 and 11, grab a C on the fifth string under the D5 chord.

✔ *BEGINNERS' TIP #3*
Think of the percussive scratches and accents in this example as the snap of a snare drum.

WEEK FOUR

Low-end chords in this lesson do more than help you dial in a rock feel. They can also enable distinctive riffs that define a song. As a case in point, play the first four measures of this week's example, using standard open chords. Sounds fine, but nothing special, right? Now try the second version, measures 5 to 8, using two-note chords on the fifth and fourth strings as shown. Use the same insistent eighth note pulse as in Week Two, but with string percussion on the unaccented beats. Sound familiar? It's from the '80s Men at Work hit "Overkill," as played these days by the songwriter Colin Hay, on acoustic guitar. (Head to YouTube to see his memorable performance on *Scrubs*.)

One of the beauties of using lean chords is that they leave you tons of dynamic range to work with. You can start off with a chugging rhythm on the bass strings and open up later in the song to big, wide chords for dramatic contrast—that's one of the most effective moves in the rock rhythm playbook.

✔ *BEGINNERS' TIP #4*
To keep the upper strings from ringing, touch them lightly with your fretting-hand index finger.

WEEK 4

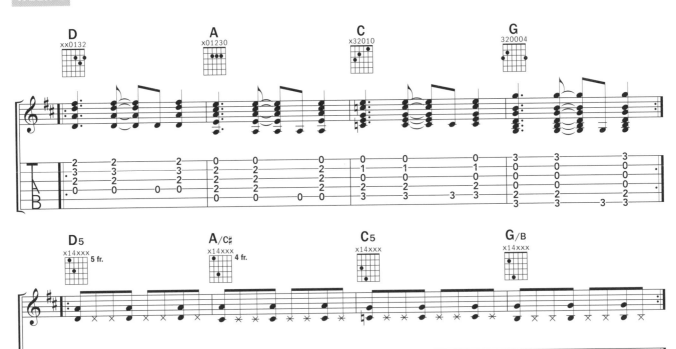

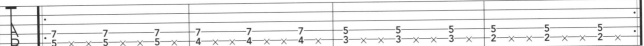

Pass It On

Learn to walk your jazz bass lines with chord accompaniment

By Ron Jackson

While studying at Berklee College of Music in Boston in the mid-1980s, I had the honor of seeing the jazz guitarist Joe Pass give a clinic. It was just him, his trusty Gibson ES-175 hollow body, and a nylon-string acoustic. Pass made those guitars sound like a full band. He demonstrated chord melody, percussive tapping, virtuoso melodic solos, and—what really got me going—walking bass lines with chord accompaniment, or "comping."

One of the best ways to learn how to play walking bass lines with chord accompaniment is to listen to jazz bassists. Another way is to understand how bass lines with chords developed. For that, you'll need to start from where it all began—that is, with Django Reinhardt and Freddie Green of the Count Basie Orchestra. Both of them played acoustic guitars and recorded that way—Reinhardt, in a small group setting, with the Manouche-style nylon-string guitar similar to a Saga Cigano; and Green, mic'd in a big-band setting, with an archtop similar to a Godin 5th Avenue or D'Angelico EXL-1.

Reinhardt and Green paved the way to playing walking bass lines on guitar with the chord shapes they used while comping in band settings. You can begin by listening to their music. After that, you'll be ready for this month's weekly workout.

In all of the examples, I have used the same chord shape and fingering, while progressively adding a walking bass line and comping pattern for subsequent weeks. Pay strict attention to the fingerings.

Use a metronome and set the tempo at about 50 bpm. Practice so that the click is on beats two and four. This imitates the hi-hat in a jazz drum kit, and will give the music a swing feel. I suggest counting the one and three between the clicks so you will be able to catch the two and four. If that's too difficult, just play on the quarter note starting at 100 bpm. I recommend using a medium pick.

In his half-century stint with the Count Basie Orchestra, Freddie Green laid the foundation for smart jazz-guitar accompaniment.

WEEK ONE

To perform walking bass lines with chords, first learn the three-note chord voicing commonly used on guitar in big bands and mainstream swing: the root, third, and seventh of the chord. For a G7 chord, the notes will be G, B, and F, omitting the fifth, or D. One G7 voicing is the G root on the sixth string, third fret; the F (which is the flat seventh note of the chord, written ♭7) on the fourth string, third fret; and the B (the third note of the chord) on the third string, fourth fret.

That chord form and its accompaniment (or, comping) is known as the "Freddie Green" style. To begin understanding this style, first familiarize yourself with these three chord voicings.

The dominant seventh chord, which has the chord intervals 1, 3, 5, ♭7. For example, in a G7 chord, the notes are G, B, D, and F.

The minor seventh chord, which has the chord intervals 1, ♭3, 5, ♭7. For example, in an Amin7 chord, the notes are A, C, E, and G.

The diminished seventh chord, which has the chord intervals 1, ♭3, ♭5, ♭7. For example, in a C#dim7 chord, the notes are C#, E, G, B♭.

Use this week to learn the jazz-blues chord progression in the key of G. It's crucial that you commit to memory these chord shapes on the fingerboard, as well as the chord progression. These shapes will be used throughout the workout.

Below is the formula for a jazz-blues in roman numerals. Roman numerals are used so you can transpose this chord progression to any key, but memorize this chord progression in the key of G.

I7	Iv7	I7	II-7-V7 of IV
Iv7	#IVdim7	I7	II-7-V7 of II
II-7	V7	I7 V7 of II	IIm7-V7 of I

Use all downstrokes on this exercise. Practice muting the unused strings and accent the two and four of each measure. Use the exact fingerings. Once you master and memorize the shapes, you will come up with your own fingerings. When strumming, make sure that you do not strum too hard. Your strums should be smooth. Practice until you can smoothly change between chords.

✔ BEGINNERS' TIP #1

Practice your bass lines with a swing feel by setting the click of your metronome as beats two and four. This imitates the hi-hat on the drum set so you can get into the groove. A walking bass line fills in the time so well that you don't even need a drummer!

WEEK TWO

It's time to add the most basic bass line: the quarter note on every four beats on the root of each chord. The easiest bass line is to play the root on every beat. Walking bass lines are almost always played as quarter notes—something known as four to the floor—and this is how you begin to create them. You also almost always play the bass notes on the fifth and sixth strings. If you try to play the bass note on the fourth string, you will be out of the bass register. Finally, you also will usually play the third and seventh of the chord on the third or fourth strings.

In Week One, you played the bass note with the third and seventh as one chord. Now, separate the bass note root from the third and seventh and create two parts. Your right hand will become very important now, because you will be using the right hand to play the two parts. This is in the realm of fingerpicking, but on a very basic level.

For this exercise, I recommend you use hybrid picking, holding the pick with your first finger and thumb to play the bass notes, and using second and third fingers to pluck the two-note third-and-seventh chord voicing. Make sure that you accent the two and four. Practice the bass line so that it sounds smoothly connected (legato) and hold the chords for their full time value.

Your ultimate goal is to sound like you are playing two separate parts.

✔ *BEGINNERS' TIP #2*
Play the bass note on every quarter note, or beat, to create a sense of "walking."

WEEK THREE
Now, you will add a real walking bass line in quarter notes with the third and seventh chord voicing playing a half note on the first and second beats, again creating two different parts. You will begin to work on the independence of both your fretting and picking hands. Practice these two parts separately—first, the bass line, then the chords—and then put them together.

Learn this walking bass line using the fingerings on the music. These specific fingerings were written to work with the chords. Notice how the walking bass line connects each chord. Also notice how I throw in an occasional open A string. Jazz bass players play open strings all the time when they walk their bass lines. It gives them a break from pressing the frets or fingerboard. Remember: always accent the bass notes on the two and four to keep that swing feel happening.

Next, practice the two-note third-and-seventh voicing. Remember the fingerings of these notes and how they fit in the chord progression. If you were to play these two-note chords in a band jamming on the blues in G, they would fit perfectly.

Now, put it all together, paying strict attention to the fingerings.

✔ **BEGINNERS' TIP #3**

Bass players use open strings all the time when walking their bass lines. Do the same on your acoustic guitar.

WEEK FOUR

This week, with the same walking bass line, play the third and seventh on top, syncopated. This requires even more independence of the fretting and picking hands.

The syncopated rhythm for the third and seventh in this example is called the Charleston rhythm (listen to Django Reinhardt's version of the song "Charleston" from the *Quintette*

du Hot Club de France album). The Charleston rhythm is a very common comping pattern in jazz.

Once you master this rhythm, put it together with the bass line. The tricky part is to mix the syncopated chords with the walking bass line.

Pay special attention to where the bass notes and chord rhythms fall into place. When you've practiced it to perfection, you'll sound like a full swing band on guitar.

✔ **BEGINNERS' TIP #4**

The goal of playing walking bass lines is to accompany yourself or others. Avoid playing a walking bass line when you're playing with a bassist, unless he or she takes a solo and you ask permission.

WEEK 4

Exploring Thirds
Enhance the sound of your playing with this all-important tool

By Sean McGowan

Many genres and guitar styles in American music are based on the all-important interval of a *third*. Melodies and solo lines are often constructed using thirds, and chord structures (for example, triads, and seventh chords) are built in thirds (sometimes known as tertian or *tertial* harmony). The type of third interval—major or minor—will determine the characteristic sound of the chord, whereas fifths and sevenths do not have the same degree of influence.

In this Weekly Workout, you'll learn different ways to map out and play thirds all over the fretboard. Lines based on thirds present great material for picking- and fretting-hand exercises, and also provide a solid foundation for melodic ideas and solos to explore in your improvising and writing.

WEEK ONE

There are two types of thirds intervals: major and minor. A major third is the distance of two whole steps; a minor third is smaller, and equal to a whole step, plus a half step. Thirds can be played on the same string (**Example 1a**) or on adjacent strings (**Example 1b**). It's important to hear, as well as see and feel, the differences between major and minor thirds. In these examples, C is the root; E♭ is the minor third, and E natural is the major third (two whole steps above C). However, these relationships are the same with any root, and they will look and feel the same on all adjacent strings, except for the G and B strings (**Ex. 1c**) due to the guitar's standard tuning.

Example 2a shows a common scale pattern for a C major scale (C D E F G A B). You can think of the notes corresponding to numbers 1, 2, 3, 4, 5, 6, and 7. If you play every other note in succession, for example, C E G B D F A, then you are moving through the scale in thirds (**Example 2b**), and you can think of the numbers as 1, 3, 5, 7, 9, 11, and 13. Note that the scale degrees 2, 4, and 6 have become 9, 11, and 13 because they are now above the octave C (8)—this is why chord symbols only feature extensions of 9, 11, and/or 13. **Example 3** illustrates an alternate pattern for a two-octave C major scale with the root on the low E string, as well as another option for moving across the strings in thirds. These examples are great guitar warm-ups, as they require some serious cross-picking to move up and down the strings. Try **Example 4**, for instance, which features the notes of C major in a combination of the thirds and scale patterns in Ex. 3, ascending and descending, for a new workout challenge. Finally, **Example 5** offers a killer workout by moving through C major in thirds, using four-note sequences. Incidentally, this particular exercise utilizes a pattern of diatonic seventh-chord arpeggios for C major, a favorite exercise among classical and jazz pianists.

✔ **BEGINNERS' TIP #1**

Play these exercises very slowly, concentrating on clarity with every note. Start out by using strict alternate picking, especially as you move across the different strings. Try just one exercise per day before moving on to the next.

WEEK 1

Examples 1a–c **Examples 2a–b**

Example 3 **Example 4**

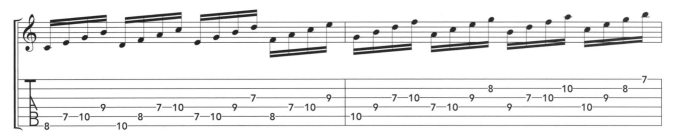

Example 5

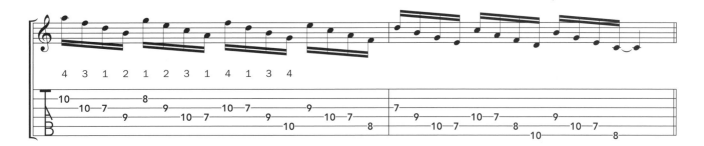

WEEK TWO

This week, you'll work with the same concepts as you did in Week One, but now applied to minor and dominant-seventh chord types. **Example 6** is the C Dorian mode (C D E♭ F G A B♭) presented in thirds. Of course, you can play any scale or mode with thirds patterns; this example uses Dorian as it works well over minor seventh chords.

Example 7 combines the ascending thirds pattern starting on the low E string, but this time it descends in the Dorian mode in sequential pairs of thirds. These combinations are sometimes known as "broken thirds," as they continuously move up and down through a scale. They are great exercises for both the fretting and picking hands. **Example 8** shows an ascending-thirds fingering for a C7 chord—using C Mixolydian (C D E F G A B♭) as the mode— starting on the fifth string. **Example 9** uses the same ascending thirds/descending broken thirds pattern you see in Ex. 7, this time over a C7 chord.

In addition to using these lines for technical workouts, spend time improvising with these concepts over chord changes in your favorite songs. **Example 10** uses the concepts from Ex. 6 and Ex. 7 over a basic Cm7–F7 chord vamp. **Example 11** features a line that would work equally well in an up-tempo bluegrass song, or medium swing blues. The melodic line over G7 features an ascending line in thirds reaching up to the ninth of the chord before coming back down the scale. Then, a combination of broken thirds is used to rappel back down the C7 chord. These thirds concepts can help you break out of the dreaded scale rut, where solos tend to sound just like scales running up and down in stepwise motion.

✔ BEGINNERS' TIP #2

In addition to the fingerings and patterns illustrated here, try coming up with your own fingerings, and write them down in a practice notebook. For example, instead of starting the pattern with your fourth finger (as in Ex. 7 and Ex. 9), you could start with your first or second finger and come up with your own patterns.

These are the fingerings for a harmonic major third (left) and a minor third (right) played on strings 1 and 2.

WEEK 2

Example 6　　　　　　**Example 7**

Cm7

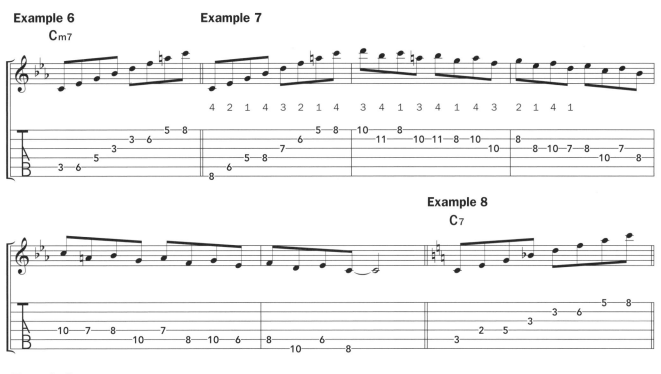

Example 8

C7

Example 9

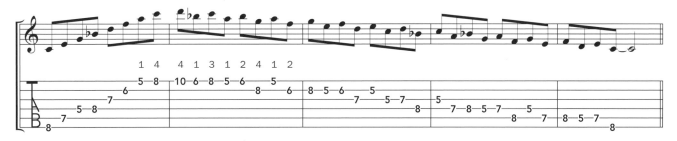

Example 10

Cm7　　　　　　F7　　　　　　Cm7

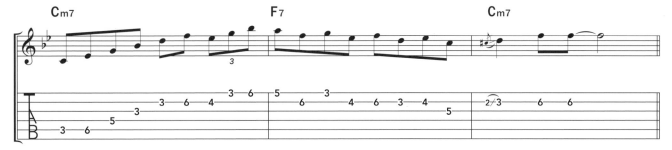

Example 11

G7　　　　　　C7

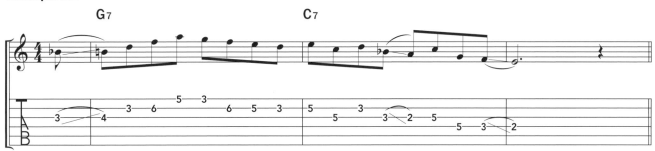

WEEK THREE

Thirds also can be played concurrently, to create a vibrant sound known as double stops. Just as broken thirds alternate between major and minor thirds, double stops will either be major or minor, depending on the combination of notes. **Example 12** harmonizes the first three notes of a C major scale, in thirds. This is a useful way to thicken up your sound, especially if you're a solo performer or the only guitarist in your group. You can also add some chromatic motion in your double-stop line to create interest, as in **Example 13**. Jerry Reed and Chet Atkins were masters of employing double stops using thirds (and fourths) in their solos, and this technique works especially well in a country-roots setting.

Example 14 shows a double-stop line in thirds over a Cm7 chord, while **Examples 15** and **16** incorporate chromatic motion, dominant ninth sounds, and sliding over dominant seventh chords. There are a few different ways to pick double stops. Since thirds will always occur on adjacent strings, you could simply articulate both strings with a flatpick. Or, you could use hybrid picking with the pick on the lower note and the middle finger sounding the top note. Many country players opt for combining a thumbpick with the index finger, especially if they have a little bit of nail, which gets closer to the sound of a pick. Finally, fingerstyle players can find a comfortable combination of the thumb with the index/middle fingers. I recommend trying and practicing all of these approaches, so you're ready for any musical situation.

✔ *BEGINNERS' TIP #3*

Explore and map out double-stop ideas for all different types of chords so that you can effortlessly drop them in and out of a single-note solo.

WEEK FOUR

The final workout shows some lead lines using all of the different techniques you've explored over the past three weeks. **Example 17** features a common chord progression (I–ii–V–I) in the key of C. The first measure starts with some double stops built from a C major scale. The second bar outlines a Dm7 chord in thirds (essentially playing a Dm7 arpeggio up and down) before moving into a broken thirds line over the G chord, and then wrapping things up with more double stops (with a little chromatic move) over the resolving C chord.

Example 18 illustrates some of the same ideas over a minor-chord vamp. Notice the melodic arc that is created over Cm7 by ascending up in thirds before cascading back down in broken thirds to resolve to where the line started. Again, a great way to prevent your solos from sounding excessively scalar is to incorporate these concepts of thirds, broken thirds, and double stops. You're still playing the notes in the scale, but presenting them in an interesting and creative way.

✔ *BEGINNERS' TIP #4*

Create several of your own melodic lines and patterns using the ideas in this lesson. Make sure to either write them down or record them so you don't forget.

WEEK 3

Example 12

Example 13

Example 14

Example 15

Example 16

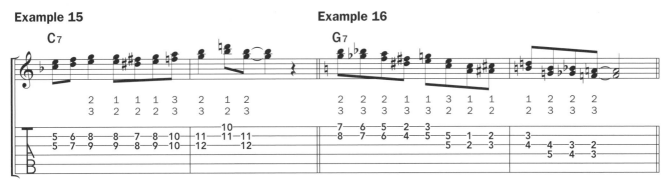

WEEK 4

Example 17

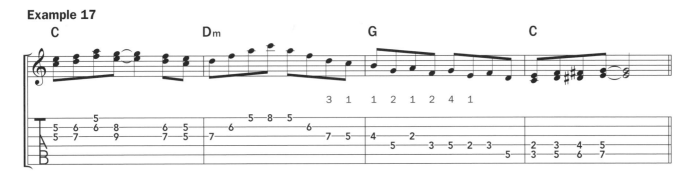

Example 18

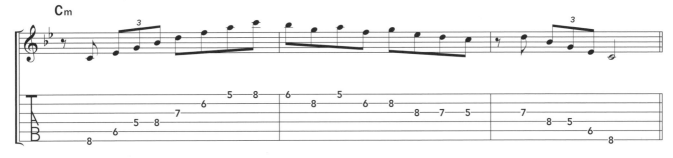

Sixths Sense
Bringing sunny sounds into shadowy harmony

By Adam Levy

If you've listened to some classic Memphis soul—Sam & Dave, Otis Redding, and so on—there's a particular way of playing harmonized melodies on the guitar that you've most certainly heard. It's a sweet, stirring sound, made by playing melodies in parallel sixths. What this means is that each melody note is supported by another note six scale degrees lower. To harmonize the melody note G in the key of G major, for example, you'd count down the scale from G until you were six scale tones lower. That lower note would be B. When you play the B and G together, you're playing a harmonic sixth. Example 1 puts this idea into action with a four-measure figure inspired by the work of Steve Cropper—the session guitarist who played on loads of Memphis soul records in the 1960s.

As you can see in **Example 1**, sixths lay easily on the guitar. That's because the instrument's standard tuning naturally features this interval. Strings 1 and 3 (E and G) happen to be tuned a sixth apart, as are strings 2 and 4 (B and D). As such, a sixth is nearly always within reach of wherever you happen to be on the fretboard. You've likely played some sixths yourself, even if you weren't thinking of them in music-theory terms.

While it's common to play sixth-based shapes in major keys—in soul and other styles—sixths are used less regularly in minor-key settings, for whatever reason. That's a shame, because melodies in this interval can be just as beautiful and evocative in minor keys. In this month's Weekly Workout, you'll study several types of minor scales and will learn to play sixths through each scale in musical ways. All of the examples in this lesson are in the key of E minor. This makes it easier to hear how the melodic ideas will sound in context, because you can hit your low E string for reference anytime. No looping pedal or backing tracks required.

WEEK ONE

There's more than one type of minor scale to study. This week, you'll get to know three of them: the natural minor, the harmonic minor, and the melodic minor. Each has its own unique character, which you'll want to learn to discern aurally. Though there's no absolute right or wrong when it comes to fretting-hand fingerings for sixths, many players finger same-fret note pairs with first-finger half barres and staggered-fret note pairs with fingers 1 and 2 (or 2 and 3). Experiment with different fingerings for each example here. Use whichever best support melodic fluidity as you move up and down the fretboard. As for your picking hand, fingerstyle or hybrid (pick and fingers) techniques tend to be most effective. **Example 2a** shows the E natural minor scale (E F♯ G A B C D) played from E to E on the first string. It's harmonized in sixths, with the lower intervals played on the third string. Play this example several times—ascending as written, as well as descending—before moving on to the next one. You'll be ready to move on once you play it without looking

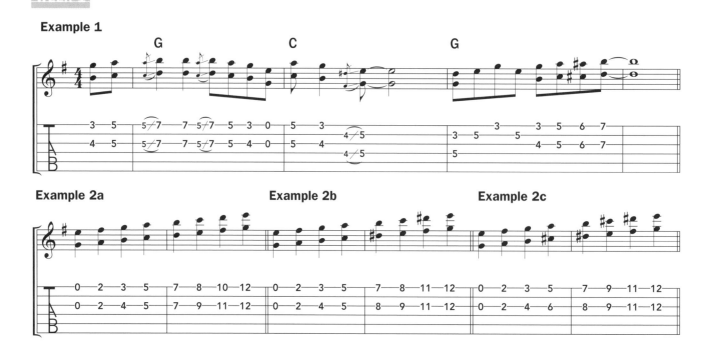

WEEK 1

Example 1

Example 2a   **Example 2b**   **Example 2c**

at the page or at your fingers. **Example 2b** is structured similarly to Ex. 2a but features the E harmonic minor scale (E F♯ G A B C D♯) instead. Again, take your time with this. Don't just sight-read it. Learn it well and be sure you can hear how it's different from Ex. 2a. You'll see the same framework once more in **Example 2c**, this time using the E melodic minor scale (E F♯ G A B C♯ D♯) in its ascending form. (When played descending, the melodic minor scale is identical to the natural minor.)

Example 3 is an ascending melodic pattern in E natural minor. Apply the same patterns to the E harmonic minor and E melodic minor scales as well. Make up some patterns of your own too—some with smallish leaps, as in Ex. 3, and some with larger leaps. As with the previous examples, patience will pay off here. Strive for accuracy and flow—not speed.

✔ *Beginners' Tip #1*

The important thing this week is learning to hear the differences between the minor scale types. Record yourself playing each scale slowly, then listen back. Train your ears, not your fingers.

WEEK TWO

This week, you'll practice these three minor scales again, using more varied melodic patterns. Such patterns are really effective when it comes to familiarizing yourself with new scales and shapes. Continue the pattern of **Example 4** as far as you comfortably can on the fretboard. Once you reach that highest point, work your way back down. Stop once you get to the open first and third strings, if you'd like, or continue the pattern on the lower strings for an extra challenge. Likewise, **Examples 5a** and **5b** may be expanded across the playable range of your guitar. Apply all four of this week's melodic patterns to the other two scales—E harmonic minor and E melodic minor—as well.

✔ *Beginners' Tip #2*

As you play each melodic pattern, use a metronome to keep your time steady. Slow tempos are fine. Convert the quarter notes here to half notes, if need be.

WEEK THREE

And now, for a completely different sound, you'll learn the ins and outs of the eight-note minor sixth diminished scale (E F♯ G A B C C♯ D♯) shown in **Example 6a**. One unusual quality of this scale is that it can be used to build a pair of chords that recur in alternate succession— Em6 and F♯ dim7, as **Example 6b** illustrates.

The next two examples show how these two chords can be used to support a simple melodic phrase. The melody is stated alone in **Example 7a**; in **Example 7b**, it's richly harmonized, using the E minor-sixth diminished scale. The harmonization method is this: Whenever the melody note is any one of the

WEEK 2

Example 3   **Example 4**

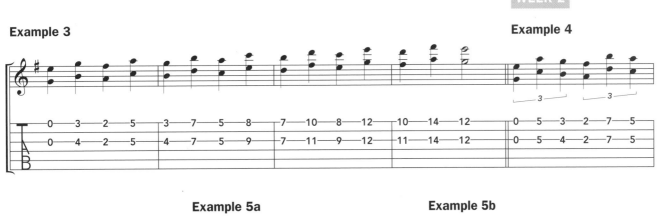

Example 5a   **Example 5b**

four chord tones of Em6 (E G B C#), use an Em6 voicing with the melody note on top; when the melody note is any one of the four chord tones of F# dim7 (F# A C E♭), use an F#dim7 voicing with the melody note on top.

How does this all relate to the sixths you've been practicing in previous weeks? You're about to find out! As you'll see in **Example 8a**, each four-note chord from Ex. 6b can be broken into two pairs of sixths. That means that you can reduce Ex. 7b from four-part harmony to two-part, while maintaining a similar quality—see **Example 8b**.

✔ *Beginners' Tip #3*
Write a short (2–4 measures) melody in the key of E minor. Use the technique you learned this week to harmonize the melody in both four and two-part settings.

WEEK FOUR

In these final figures, you'll learn to apply the previous weeks' concepts to a different sort of minor scale—minor pentatonic (in the key of E minor, once again, for ease and convenience), shown in **Example 9a**. Because of this scale's five-note construction (E G A B D), it's not possible to harmonize every scale tone in sixths. While this may seem to be a downside, it's actually a plus—because it will lead to some interesting non-parallel harmony.

The first interval pair in **Example 9b** is a sixth (G and E). The next two pairs are sevenths (A and G, B and D), followed by another sixth (D and B), another seventh (E and D), and finally a sixth (G and E). Play this example a few times to familiarize yourself with this unusual sound, focusing your ears on the top line first. Then play it again and see if you can

focus on the bottom line. Finally, play the example once more and try to hear both lines simultaneously.

Example 9c starts with the interval pair of a fifth (A and E). Most of the other pairs here are fifths as well. Only the B-and-G pair (measure 1, beat 2, and measure 3, beat 2) are sixths. Still, this harmonization is a not-too-distant cousin of Ex. 9b and is worth exploring as you study minor-key sixths.

Example 10 is a folkish melody that utilizes the harmonies from Ex. 9b. The previous examples have all been played over the I chord. This one brings a couple of other harmonies into the fold, as indicated by the chord symbols.

✔ *Beginners' Tip #4*
If the character of Week Four's examples appeals to you, try composing your own pentatonic etude—in E minor or any other minor key. New musical concepts tend to stick more permanently when your creative "muscles" are engaged.

TAKE IT TO THE NEXT LEVEL

While all of the examples in this lesson are presented in the key of E minor, be sure to practice this material in other keys as well. The next logical step would be A minor, because you can use the open A as a bass-note reference (as you did with the low E) while playing sixths on strings 1 and 3 or 2 and 4—as shown in the example here. But don't stop there. There are 12 minor keys in total. Get to know the scales and intervals in all of them. If there's a minor song that you love to play, practice it in every key—sans capo. When you can easily play scales and intervals in any key and can apply this lesson's concepts to a favorite song in any key, your level of fluency with sixths will be very high.

WEEK 3

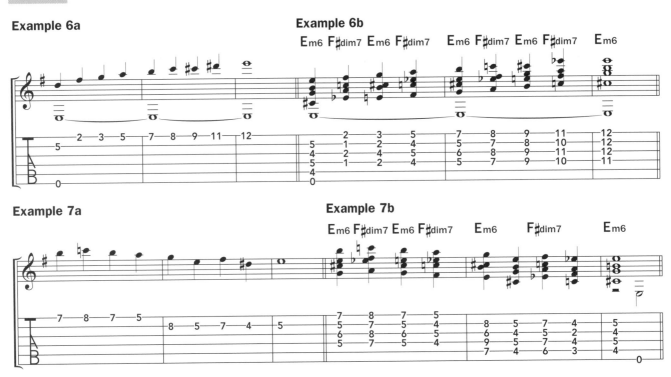

Example 6a

Example 6b

Example 7a

Example 7b

Example 8a

let ring throughout

WEEK 4

Example 8b　　　　　　　　　　　　　　　　　　　　**Example 9a**

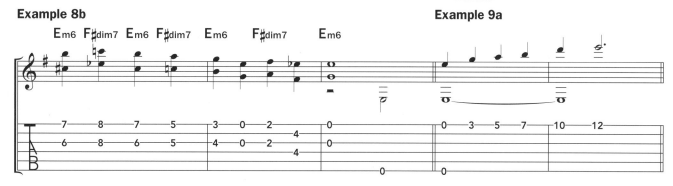

Example 9b　　　　　　　　**Example 9c**　　　　　　　　**Example 10**

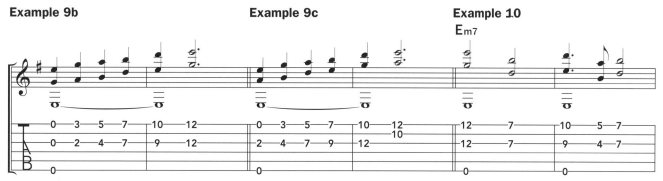

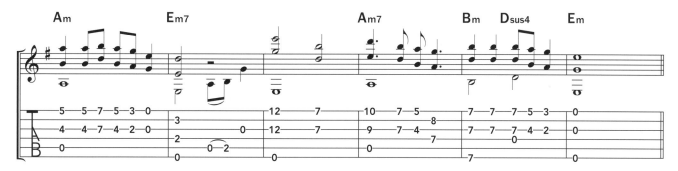

Take It to the Next Level

Shape Shifting
Play chords built from pentatonic scales

By Sean McGowan

Most guitarists, regardless of ability or genre, are familiar with playing pentatonic scales. Countless songs, melodies, solos, and classic riffs are based on the sound and structure of the pentatonic scale, which is literally any scale with five notes. However, most musicians refer to the major- pentatonic scale, which is built from scale degrees 1-2-3-5-6; or, a major scale without the fourth and seventh degrees. The minor pentatonic scale (1-♭3-4-5-♭7) is an inversion of the major pentatonic (from the fifth note, or scale degree 6), and is often the first scale that guitarists learn on the fretboard.

The pentatonic scale is popular in musical cultures throughout the world for a number of reasons. By omitting the fourth and seventh, the inherent dissonance created by half steps and the tritone interval (between the fourth and seventh) are removed. As a result, every note in a major pentatonic scale sounds consonant. For this reason, wind chimes are often tuned to pentatonic scales. This scale is popular for beginning improvisers for the same reason—every note sounds great!

Here are some exercises to help you play chords that are built from pentatonic scales. Pentatonic chord structures are relatively uncommon compared to their scalar counterparts. But they offer unique and beautiful sounds that will create interesting textures, whether you're writing a song, playing rhythmic chord fills in a tune, looking to add colorful textures to fill out your lead lines, or simply looking for a good physical workout and way to reinforce your knowledge of the fretboard.

WEEK ONE

Start by reacquainting yourself with the major-pentatonic scale. **Example 1** shows a common fingering for a C major pentatonic. In the same way that an Am chord is the relative minor to C major, so is the Am pentatonic scale shown in **Example 2**; it is the exact same scale as C major pentatonic, starting on the sixth degree, or note (A). With this in mind, you can now use pentatonic scales and chords for both major chords and minor chords down a minor third interval. For example, C and Am have this relationship, as well as G and Em, D and Bm, B♭ and Gm, etc.

Before you start applying three- and four-note chord structures, work through double-stops using the pentatonic. **Examples 3** and **4** offer fingerings for the C major—or A minor—pentatonic scale in double-stops starting on two different intervals. Again, notice that every note sounds consonant and sweet. Also, they create unique intervals due to the large skip in the scale (between the third and fifth degrees); as a result, the intervals change between thirds and fourths [Ex. 3] and fifths and sixths [Ex. 4].

Example 5 shows a possible lead line or fill using double-stops from the C major pentatonic scale, which works over C and Am chords. Play through this example slowly and hone in on the different sounds created by some of these two-note structures. There is an element of familiarity, yet it yields some interesting chords and shapes such as the last chord in the example. **Example 6** illustrates the same type of lead idea using double-stops. However, this time the chord progression moves from C to Gm. To fit our lines over these changes, use C/Am pentatonic for the first bar, and B♭/Gm pentatonic for the second bar over the Gm chord. All of these patterns are movable; therefore, you can take our C/Am shapes and simply move them down two frets to access the B♭/Gm pentatonic shapes. Try playing these examples fingerstyle and hybrid using the pick and fingers.

WEEK 1

Example 1
C

Example 2
Am

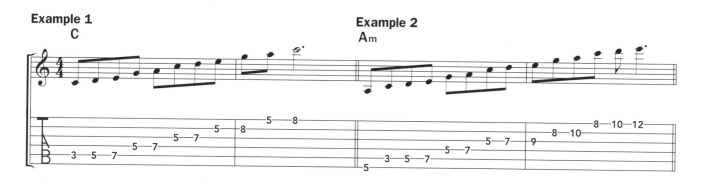

Example 3
C

Example 4
Am

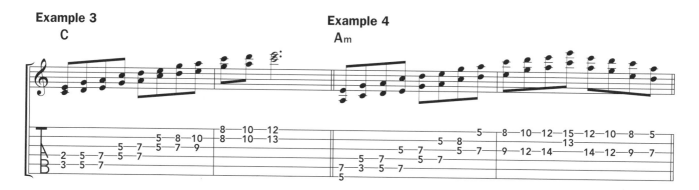

Example 5
C   Am

Example 6
C   Gm

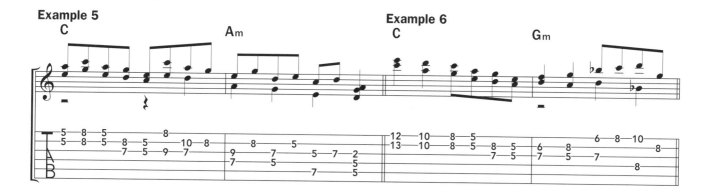

WEEK TWO

Now you're ready to explore some three- and four-note structures, thereby creating chords built from the pentatonic scale. The first three examples this week (**Examples 7–9**) illustrate chords using only notes from the C/Am pentatonic scale, starting with a unique intervallic structure. The first example starts with a basic C major triad. Yet, because there are only five notes in the scale, the chords shift from common triads to unique voicings comprised of second and fourth intervals. These sound more like little chord structures a keyboardist might use, and will fit the bill perfectly if you're looking for new, compact chord voicings in a tune.

Example 10 also moves through the C/Am pentatonic scale, this time with four notes. These are a little more diffi-cult to play than the three-note versions, but they provide a great workout for the fretting hand. Remember, you don't have to always play scales for a workout–getting in and out of complex chords is also a workout!

Example 11a shows a chordal line built on the previous patterns. The subsequent examples illustrate how this same line will work over C (**Example 11b**), Am, and also related chords that would commonly be associated with these tonalities. For example, **Example 11c** uses Em and Am chords, while **Example 11d** the line over Dm, Am, and finally, C chords. Try using a looper or recording device to play these types of chordal ideas over different notes and chords; there are lots of great sounds to explore and dis-cover in these structures.

WEEK 2

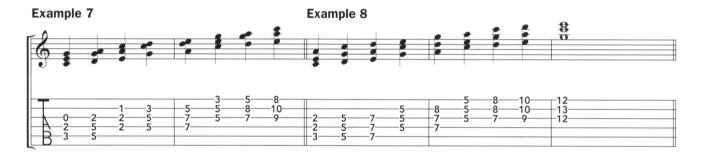

Example 7   Example 8

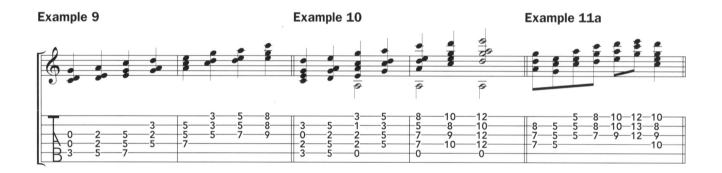

Example 9   Example 10   Example 11a

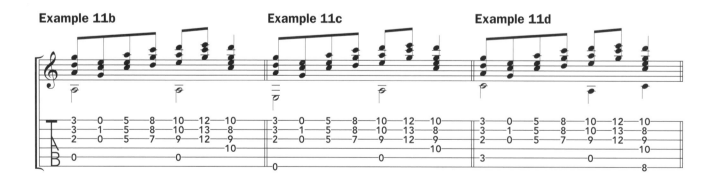

Example 11b   Example 11c   Example 11d

WEEK THREE

Take some of these pentatonic chord ideas and apply them to songwriting, arranging, and lead situations. Remember, the idea is to create new yet familiar-sounding lines and chord structures from only the five notes of the scale. **Example 12** shows a simple melody or lead line from the C/Am pentatonic scale, supported with little three-note chord structures. Try playing the example with and without the accompanying chords, and notice the difference. Some of these structures—based on their design using second and fourth intervals—almost sound like an altered/ modal tuning such as DADGAD, but you can easily resolve the music with a common C chord, as in this example. **Example 13**

uses the same scale, but in the context of a fingerstyle pattern and progression. This example could work as an excerpt from an instrumental piece or as a foundation for a song with lyrics. Singer-songwriters might find this concept especially attractive if they are looking for alternative chord voicings in standard tuning, without straying too far from the sound of the chord itself.

The next two examples show possibilities in a lead setting. **Example 14** features a little melodic break in G minor using structures from the Bb/Gm pentatonic. **Example 15** is the same idea, with a little hybrid picking counterpoint line in the last two bars. These will work great in any kind of setting, offering a familiar blues-oriented sound, with unique chordal support.

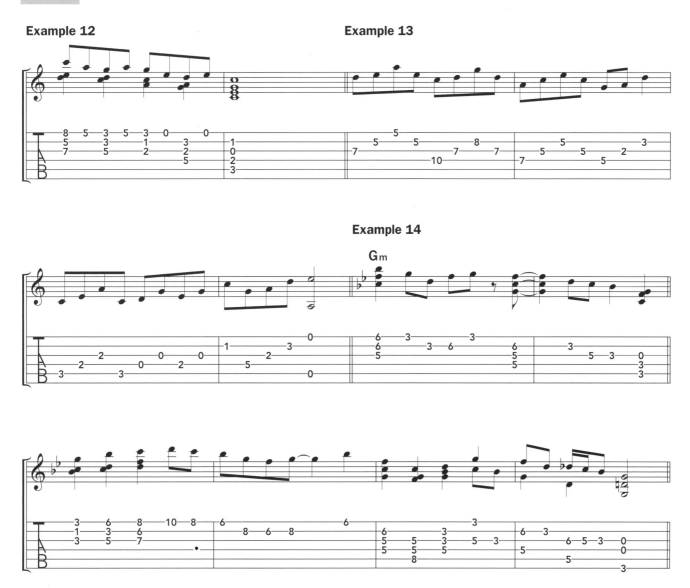

WEEK FOUR

Now, look at how to use different scales over one chord, employing a common substitution technique. Here's the essential concept: over any minor chord, you can use a minor pentatonic scale based on the root and/or the fifth of the chord. For example, if you are playing over an Am chord, you can use both Am and Em pentatonic scales as the basis for lead and rhythm lines. If you want to add a little more modal complexity (think Allman Bros. vamps) you also can use the minor pentatonic on the second degree. That would be a Bm pentatonic if you're still in Am. The Bm pentatonic (B D E F♯ A) creates a Dorian type of modal sound, due to the F♯ on top of the Am. If you're playing a song that has long sections of just one chord, this is a great way to add some interest without going too far outside of the tonality.

You can easily apply this lead substitution concept to rhythm using pentatonic chords. **Example 16** illustrates pentatonic chord patterns for Am, Bm, and Em, all of which work beautifully over an Am chord. If you're playing in another key,

simply transpose the formula of root, second, and fifth of that key. For instance, if you're playing in Gm, use Gm, Am, and Dm.

Use these substitutions over major chords, too. They will work just fine over the relative major of the minor key you're in. For example, your Am chords (as well as Bm and Em) will work great over C, which is the relative major of Am as shown in **Example 17**. **Example 18** shows structures built from the G/Em pentatonic (first two bars) and D/Bm pentatonic (second two bars), all of which work over G or Em chords. In this example, think of Em as the root, and Bm as the fifth. G major is the relative major of Em, just like C is the relative major of Am.

EXTRA CREDIT

There are many other pentatonic scales besides the major (and minor) explored in this lesson. For extra credit, work through two additional pentatonic scales, the Dorian pentatonic (aka "♭3 pentatonic") and Dominant pentatonic, both based on and named after modes of the major scale.

WEEK 4

Example 16
Am

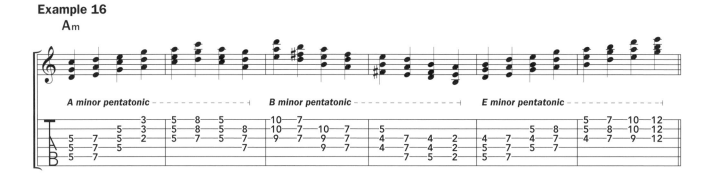

Example 17
C
Example 18

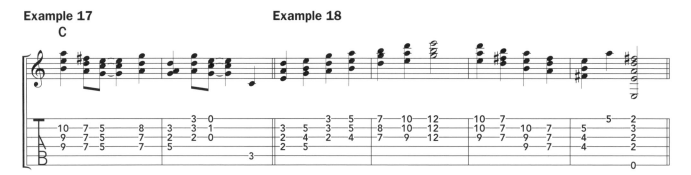

Example 19
Dorian Pentatonic
Cm

Example 20

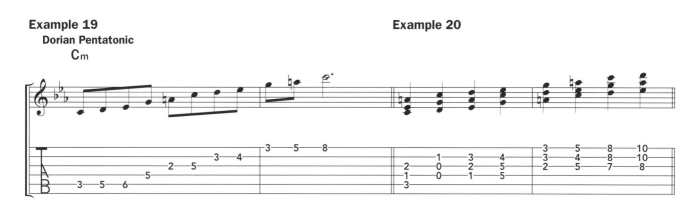

Example 21
Cm

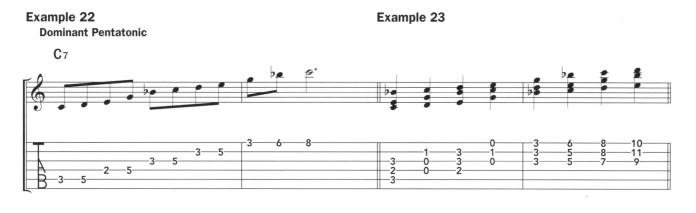

Example 22
Dominant Pentatonic
C7

Example 23

Example 24

Horizontal Harmonies
Using melodic tools to express chord changes

By Adam Levy

Guitarists tend to think of harmony and melody as two distinctly different musical elements. For most players, harmony consists of the standard chord grips. Melodies are played one note at a time and are usually related to familiar scale patterns. While those conceptions aren't incorrect, there are ways of making harmonies more melodic, and vice versa.

To give your melodies more harmonic lucidity, you can emphasize essential chord tones on the strong beats (beats 1 and 3 in 4/4 time) of each measure and use other scale degrees on the weaker beats. To make your harmonies more melodic, you can play two-part counterpoint in lieu of stock chords. These integrative approaches—which you'll learn in this month's Weekly Workout—can keep your playing fresh and dynamic in any musical style.

WEEK ONE

One way to learn how melody playing can be made more harmonically clear is to study the repertoire of a non-chordal instrument, such as the violin. (Chords can be played on the violin, but the instrument is melodic by design.) Traditional Irish fiddle tunes—jigs, reels, and hornpipes—are a great place to start, because many of the tunes are easily transferable to the guitar fretboard.

In this week's lesson, you'll play "St. Anne's Reel," as shown in **Example 1**. It's meant to be played at a brisk 200 bpm, but take it more slowly at first if need be. Once you have Ex. 1 under your fingers, repeat the entire tune several times, until the melody becomes so familiar that you're barely reading the music at all.

Record yourself playing Ex. 1 along with a metronome. As you listen back to your recording, play along using the chord symbols shown. There should be no surprises, as the melody is already telegraphing the harmony quite clearly. In next week's workout, you'll learn to write your own harmony-rich melody.

✔ *BEGINNERS' TIP #1*

Remember those Magic Eye posters that were popular in the early '90s? At first glance, they looked like random colored dots. But when you learned how to adjust your gaze, 3-D images would appear. Studying a new melody can be sort of like that. You have to get past just playing the right notes in order to really hear the melody—and, hence, the harmony.

J.S. Bach was a master of implying harmony through elegant horizontal lines.

WEEK 1

Example 1

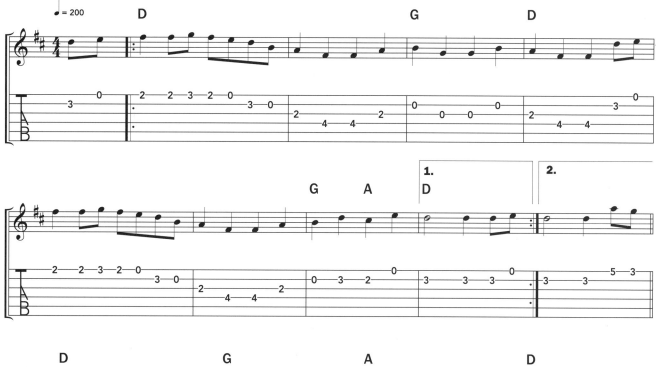

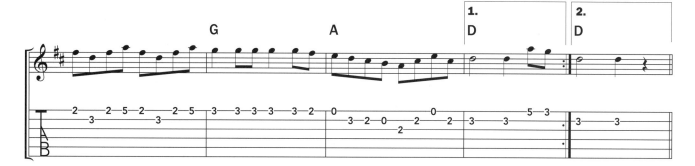

WEEK TWO

Now that you can play Ex. 1, it's time take a look under the hood. **Example 2a** shows the guide tones at the heart of that tune. Guide tones are fundamental chord tones. In folk music, that usually means the root, third, or fifth; in jazz and other styles, the seventh is considered a guide tone as well. These tones are typically placed on the strong beats of each measure. The guide tones in Ex. 2a are taken directly from Ex. 1's melody. The first and third notes of each measure there have been converted to half notes here. Your assignment this week is to create your own reel-style melody based on these guide tones. You don't need to add

many more notes to bring the melody to life. Compare Ex. 2a with Ex. 1 and you'll see. You may find it helpful to closely (or exactly) copy the rhythms from Ex. 1 (use eighths in your melody where you see eighths in Ex. 1, and so on). As this piece is in the key of D major, use notes from the D major scale as scalar connectors between the guide tones. Example 2b is given as a model.

✔ *BEGINNERS' TIP #2*

Once you familiarize yourself with a guide-tone melody like Example 2a, let it do the work for you. You need only add a few scalar passing tones to create your own tune.

Example 2a

Example 2b

WEEK THREE

Irish fiddle tunes aren't the only part of violin repertoire that use melodic lines to convey shifting harmonies. In the early 1700s, J.S. Bach composed his *Sonatas and Partitas for Solo Violin*, which became a cornerstone of the classical repertoire. Though some movements of these pieces include three- and four-part chords, the bulk of the work is made up of single-note melodies.

Example 3 is an excerpt from the Presto movement of Bach's *Sonata No. 1 in G minor*. Although the implied chord progression here (shown above the staff) is more sophisticated than those in the previous examples, the guide-tone principle can be seen here as well—that is, you'll find essential chord tones on the strong beats. (The strong and weak beats in 3/8 meter are less predictable than in 4/4 because 3/8 measures may be subdivided into two groups of three 16ths or three groups of two 16ths. In the case of the former, the first and fourth 16ths will be considered the strong beats; in the latter, the first, third, and fifth 16ths will be strong.)

One new musical element here is the use of sequencing—the repetition of melodic motifs across changing harmonies. Sequencing can be a very effective tool for extending melodic ideas through several measures of music. In this example, measures 3 and 4 are sequenced from the motif in measure 2, and the two-measure motif in bars 5 and 6 is sequenced through the four measures that follow. Another two-measure motif occurs in measures 10 and 11 and is sequenced through the end of this example.

Once you can play Ex. 3 as written, experiment! Trace the given chord progression with your own one- and two-measure 16th-note motifs.

✔ BEGINNERS' TIP #3

With its perpetual motion and breakneck tempo, Example 3 may be intimidating. Cut it into shorter phrases—just three or four measures each—at first, then stitch the phrases together once you can play each with confidence.

WEEK 3

Example 3

♪. = 168

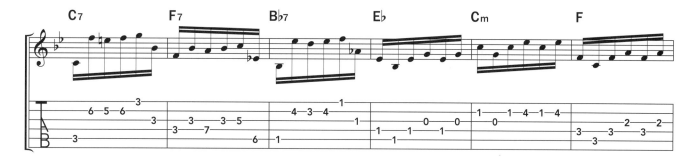

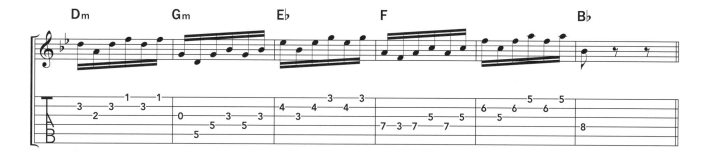

WEEK FOUR

This week you'll learn how to make your harmonies more melodic by employing two-part counterpoint as an alternative to common chord shapes. To explain counterpoint, a few fundamental terms must be defined. When two notes move the same intervallic distance in the same direction (up or down), that's called *parallel* motion. (See **Example 4a**.) Two notes moving different distances in the same direction is called *similar* motion (**Example 4b**). *Contrary* motion is when two notes move in opposite directions (**Example 4c**). When one note moves and the other stays, that's *oblique* motion (**Example 4d**). Now look at **Example 5**. Can you find examples of all four types of contrapuntal motion?

Record yourself playing Ex. 5 along with a metronome or other steady timekeeper. Listen back—a few times, or more. See if you can begin to hear two individual melodic lines distinctly, as well as hearing them as a harmonic whole. Compose your own blues counterpoints—in G or other keys—making sure to include all four motion types. Once you've written a few of these, try

improvising contrapuntally in real time. It's definitely not easy, but trial-and-error is part of the learning process. Keep at it.

✔ BEGINNERS' TIP #4

Practice playing just the upper notes of Week Four's dyads at first. Next, just the lower. When you finally put them both together, you should still be able to hear each melody distinctly.

TAKE IT TO THE NEXT LEVEL

Here's an example based on the first seven measures of the jazz standard "All the Things You Are." It incorporates the contrapuntal concept from Week 4 (measures 1–2), the sequencing concept from Week 3 (measures 3–4), and the guide-tone concept from Week 2 (measures 6–7). Be sure to continue exploring the harmony/melody connection in a variety of keys (major and minor), tempos, and time signatures. And, as always, take what you learn into all areas of the fretboard—including the open strings, the uppermost fret positions, and natural harmonics. Leave no musical stone unturned.

WEEK 4

Examples 4a–d

Example 5

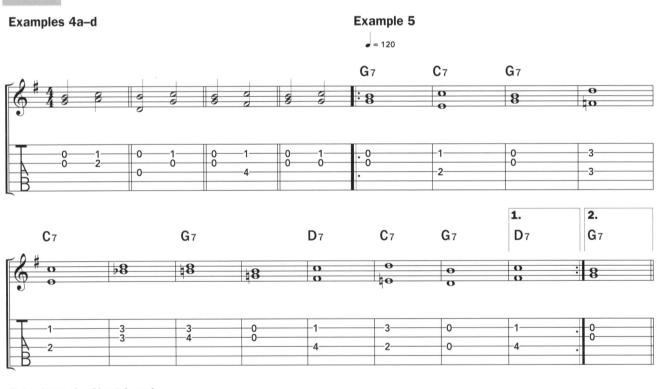

Take It to the Next Level

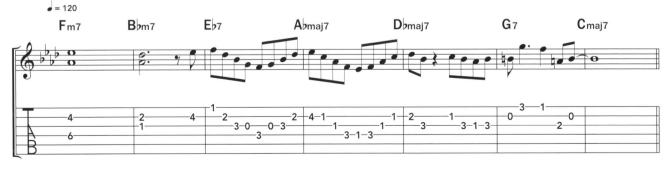

Spice Up Your Playing
An introduction to jazz reharmonization

By Ron Jackson

Jazz is packed with harmonies that can sound foreign to those not in the know. But with the knowledge of a few basic principles, it all starts to make sense. What jazz players are often doing is reharmonizing basic chord progressions common to different popular styles—progressions that you likely already know—and using substitute chords to add color and complexity.

If you're not a jazz musician, learning jazz harmony might not seem particularly compelling. But whether you play folk, rock, country blues, Celtic fingerstyle, or anything else, knowing how jazz harmony works and borrowing from it now and then can only make your music more interesting, while enhancing your musicianship. With that in mind, dig in to this primer on various harmonic techniques.

WEEK ONE

In order to understand chord substitution, you should first be familiar with basic diatonic harmony—chords formed from the notes of a given scale. Take a moment to study **Example 1**, which shows the triads (three-note chords) built from the notes of the C major scale and **Example 2**, depicting seventh chords derived from the scale. You'll be using these Roman numerals later in this workout; note that uppercase numerals represent major chords and lowercase minor chords. Now let's get into some substitutions. **Example 3** is a basic progression in the key of C containing the I, IV, and V chords (C, F, and G7). To make the progression more interesting, in **Example 4**, on beat 3 of bar 1, you'll substitute the C chord with a C7. On beat 3 of the next bar, in place of the F major chord, you'll play an F minor, lending an interesting harmonic color.

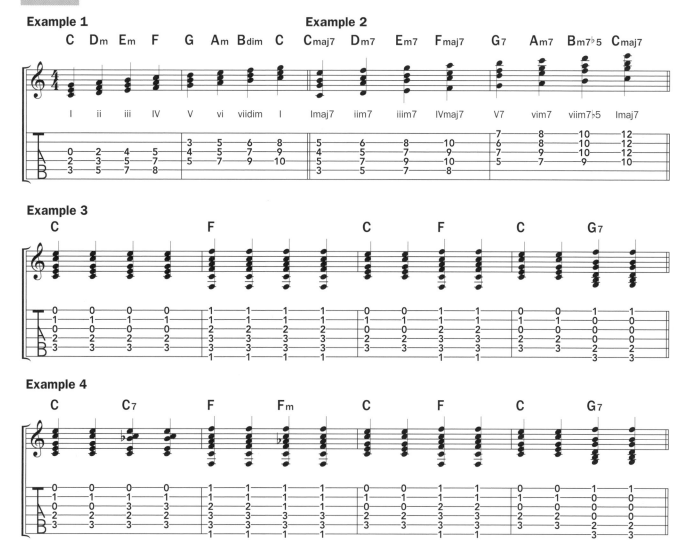

WEEK 1

Example 1

Example 2

Example 3

Example 4

In **Example 5**, throw some bass notes other than roots into the mix for even more harmonic flavor. For instance, on beat 3 of bar 1, play the C7 chord's third, E, as the lowest note, leading smoothly up to the F in the following measure. Now, to hear how your I–IV–V progression has been transformed over the last few exercises, compare Ex. 5 to Ex. 3.

✔ *BEGINNERS' TIP #1*

To build a strong base for your reharmonization skills, memorize the triads and seventh chords within on all major scales. Start in C major and practice in all keys through the cycle of fifths.

WEEK TWO

This week you'll treat a I–vi–ii–V progression, the bedrock of so many jazz and popular songs, to a variety of reharmonizations. Begin with the basic progression, shown in the key of C major in **Example 6**. Next, in **Example 7**, replace the I chord (Cmaj7) with the iii (Em7). In **Example 8**, you'll use another common substitution—the V7 of ii. Instead of playing the vi chord Am, which occurs naturally in C major, you'll play an A7, the V7 of Dm7.

Combine the substitutions in Ex. 7 and Ex. 8 to arrive at **Example 9**, which creates a pair of descending ii–V progressions (Em7–A7 and Dm7–G7)—an essential jazz move. Turn the minor-seventh chords into dominant sevenths (**Example 10**) and you'll have a series of seventh chords travel-ing counterclockwise on the circle of fifths. Astute readers will know this particular sequence of chords as that used in the bridge of "rhythm changes"—named after the Gershwin tune "I Got Rhythm," one of the most common forms in jazz.

In **Example 11** we substitute the A7 and G7 chords with E♭7 and D♭7. This move is known as tritone substitution—the root of the E♭7 chord (E♭) is a tritone, or three steps from that of the A7 chord, and ditto for the roots of the D♭7 and G7 chords. If that sounds confusing, spend a minute with **Example 12**, which gets into the concept more deeply. In bar 1 you'll find a G7 chord and its tritone substitution, D♭7. As demonstrated in the second bar, these two chords have two notes in common—F, which is the seventh of G7 and the third of D♭7, and B/C♭, which is the third of G7 and the flatted seventh of D♭7. Put it all together by adding the roots (G and D♭) in the third measure.

For good measure, subject the original I–vi–ii–V to one last variation. As directed in **Example 13**, keep the tritone sub on beat 3 of each measure, but revert to the I and ii chords (Cmaj7 and Dm7). Note the smoothly descending bass line (E♭–D–D♭) between the last three chords.

✔ *BEGINNERS' TIP #2*

In progressions that you already know, try adding extra notes to the chords, for enhanced harmonic color. Also try inserting diatonic chords between the chords in a stock progression.

Example 5

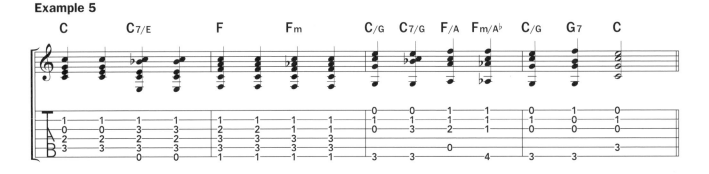

WEEK 2

Example 6   **Example 7**   **Example 8**

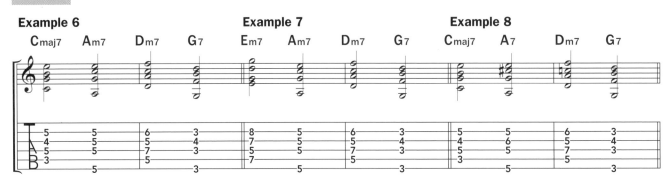

WEEK THREE

In some instances, you can think of complex-sounding chords in simple terms: as triads over bass notes. For example, the first chord in bar 1 of **Example 14** is typically labeled as Cmaj9, but you can get the same sound by playing a G triad (G B D) over the note C, as the next voicing illustrates. The second measure shows you how to use the Cmaj9 chord in a ii–V–I progression—another building block of jazz—in the key of C.

You can also think of a minor-seventh chord as a triad over a bass note. Bar 1, beat 1 of **Example 15** shows a typical Dm7 chord in fifth position, while the chord on beat 3 shows that a Dm7 chord is equivalent to an F triad (F A C). Try plugging this chord into the ii–V–I progression, as shown in bar 2.

If you're not a jazzer, then you might not know what to do if someone asks you to play, say, a 13♭9 chord. But this altered dominant chord, too, can be played as a triad. The first bar of **Example 16** shows what happens when you play an E triad over a G bass note (with the addition of the G chord's flatted seventh, F), and the second bar places the resulting chord in the ii–V–I progression. Notice how between the first two chords the F triad on strings 1–3 moves down neatly by half step to the E triad.

✔ **BEGINNERS' TIP #3**

Get to know more complex chords by seeing them as triads played over bass notes—for example, view a Gmaj9 chord as a D triad over the note G.

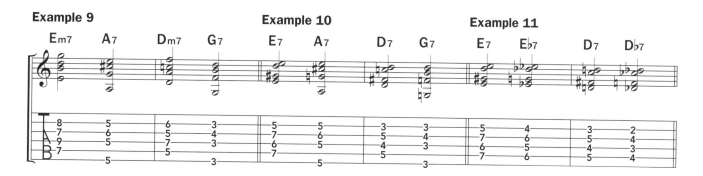

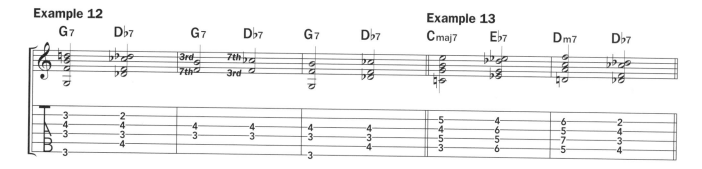

WEEK 3

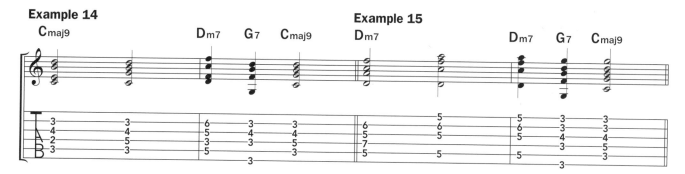

WEEK FOUR

This week we'll explore various ways to spice up single chords, rather than chords in progression. If you're faced with a dominant seventh chord, for instance, you might flatten its fifth or raise it, as shown in **Example 17**, which creates a nice dynamic tension in the sound. In **Example 18**, do the same with an Fmaj7 chord for new harmonic colors.

Another way of making a chord more interesting is to move one of its voices around in what's known in jazz as a line cliché or chromatic cliché. In **Example 19**, start with a plain old C chord, then move its second-highest voice, on string 3, around by a half step to form a C–Caug–C6–Caug progression. **Example 20** is based on the same idea, but the note that moves around is the highest voice.

The same concept is illustrated on a Dm chord in **Example 21**, where movement on string 2 results in a colorful Dm–Dm(maj7)–Dm7–Dm6 progression. In **Example 22**, the notes on string 3 are shifted around to create a Dm–Dm(#5)–Dm6–Dm(#5) move, recalling the James Bond theme.

Once you've absorbed all the chord-substitution and reharmonization ideas in this workout, try it again in other keys. Take the concepts, apply them to your own music, and you'll be playing with new depth and excitement.

✔ **BEGINNERS' TIP #4**

Apply line clichés—moving voices—on phrases that sit on the same chord for one or more measures at a time.

WEEK 4

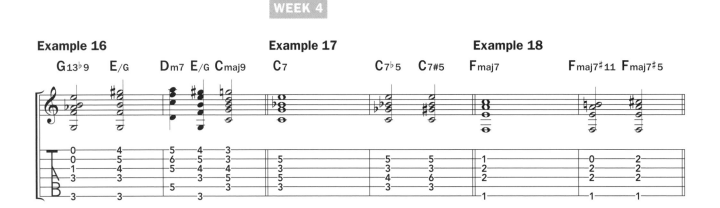

Example 16 · Example 17 · Example 18

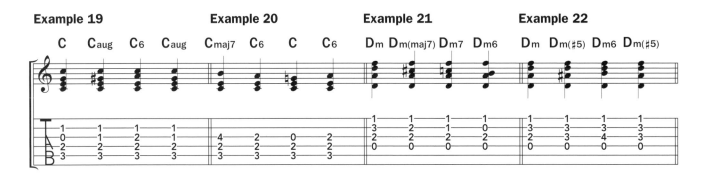

Example 19 · Example 20 · Example 21 · Example 22

How to Harmonize in a Chet Atkins Style
An introduction to playing chord melodies

By Ron Jackson

Learning to play chord-melody style—that is, expressing melodies in chords rather than single notes—is a formidable and valuable skill. While the approach has been seen most commonly in the works of jazz and jazz-informed musicians such as Earl Klugh and Chet Atkins, it can be used to add new dimensions to virtually any style. This Weekly Workout will show you everything you need to get started harmonizing melodies, through assorted treatments of the classic tunes "London Bridge is Falling Down" and "Billy Boy."

WEEK ONE

A prerequisite to playing in the chord-melody style is for you to know a given melody inside out, in both your ears and your fingers—in different positions and, ideally, different keys. Having a firm grasp on the melody will allow you to harmonize it more easily. Start with the melody of "London Bridge," written in the key of G major in **Example 1**. Play it as notated, and then experiment with some of your own fingerings.

In **Example 2**, you'll flesh out the melody with some basic open chords, falling under every other note in bars 1–3 and all of the notes in bar 4. It's helpful to know the function of each melody note. For instance, the first note, D, is the fifth of the G chord; the second note, E, is the sixth, etc. Before you play the example, determine the functions of the rest of the melody notes.

When you work through the example, whether fingerstyle or hybrid picking (pick and fingers), it's important to play the melody notes louder than the other chord tones by attacking them with greater force—but not too much. Be patient, as it might take some time to get the hang of this.

WEEK 1

Example 1

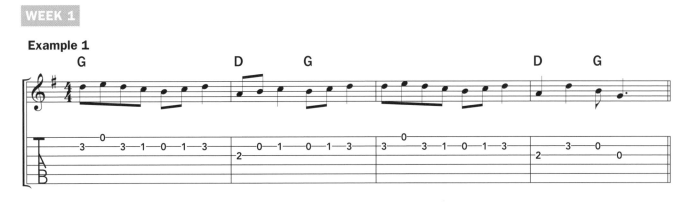

Example 2

Example 3

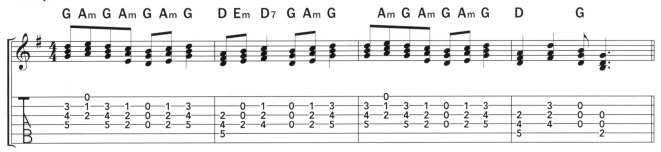

You'll place a chord under every melody note in **Example 3**, which uses a different approach to harmony, containing mostly diatonic triads (falling strictly within the key of G) instead of the basic I–V (G–D) progression. Note that the voices (notes) of the chords move entirely in parallel motion. Keep your fretting hand close to the strings when switching between chords. When playing chords up and down the fingerboard, slide your fretting hand fingers into the next chord.

✔ BEGINNERS' TIP #1

In the chord-melody style, play the melody so it's louder than the rest of the notes in a chord by applying more pressure with your pick or finger.

WEEK TWO

You don't always need to play the melody on top of the chord. In **Example 4**, it's placed in the second note from the top voice in each chord. The occasional inversion—a note other than the root in the bass—helps keep the movement between chords smooth. For instance, in bar 1, on beat 3, the G chord's third, B, appears in the bass and ascends neatly by a half step to connect with the C chord's root, C, on the "and" of 3.

This example is trickier to play, since the melody is in an inner voice. Try using fingerpicking or hybrid picking for this example, taking care to apply more pressure to the melody notes. To make the chords sound smoothly connected, hold each note for as long as possible. For instance,

WEEK 2

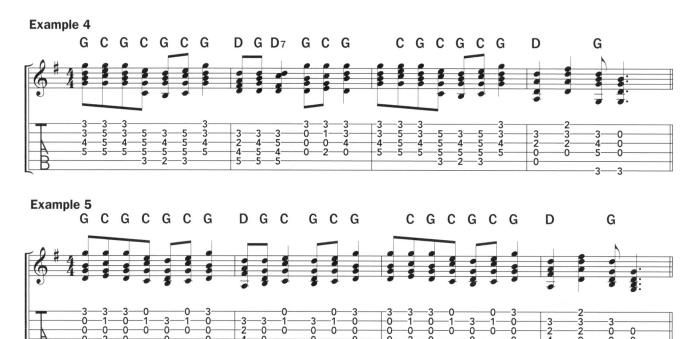

in bar 2, fret the first-string G with you fourth finger; keep that finger in place as you add your first and second fingers to play the C chord.

In **Example 5**, the melody is moved to the lowest note of each chord. Accent each melody bass note by picking slightly harder against each note while rolling your pick or fingers across the strings. Be sure to mute unused strings.

✔ *BEGINNERS' TIP #2*

Fret-hand efficiency is important in chord-melody playing. Use the least amount of motion between chords while making sure to fret them cleanly.

WEEK THREE

This week you'll kick things up a notch with a jazz-approved, chord-melody arrangement of "Billy Boy." But first, just as you did with "London Bridge," familiarize yourself with the melody, written in the key of B♭ major and including only the I and V chords (B♭ and F7, respectively) in **Example 6**. Once you know "Billy Boy" in your sleep, proceed to **Example 7**, in which a chord falls squarely on each beat. As opposed to the previous exercises, you're now entirely in seventh-chord territory, with lots of interesting harmonic moves. In bar 1, for instance, instead of just the I chord (B♭), you've got a I–vi–ii–V progression (B♭maj7–Gm7–Cm7–F7).

WEEK 3

Example 6

Example 7

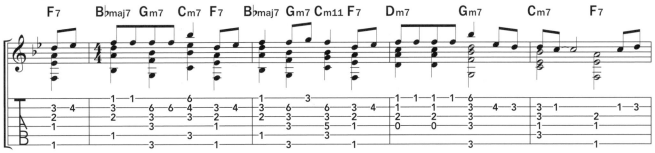

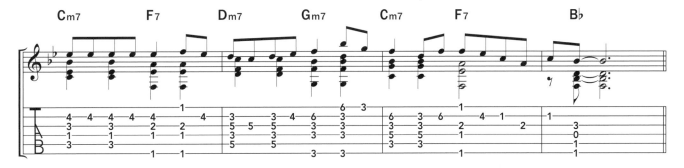

Don't worry about these labels if you're not a theory nerd—half of the battle in learning the chord-melody style is to focus on the technical aspects on the guitar. Practice the example one bar at a time until you've polished off the whole thing. Also, try to memorize the music, so that you can really focus on making this example sing.

✔ *BEGINNERS' TIP #3*

Always know the function of the melody in a chord. For example, on a C chord, the melody note E is the third.

WEEK FOUR

As long as you can clearly hear the melody when you're playing in the chord-melody style, then you can throw in the kitchen sink when it comes to harmonic choices. You'll do just that this week with a radically re-harmonized rendition of "Billy Boy" (**Example 8**). A whole method book could be devoted to the harmonic techniques at play here, but again, if you're not yet up to speed, don't worry too much about the music theory in learning this example.

But if you are into theory, here are a few highlights: There are the chromatic passing chords—on bar 1, beat 2, Bdim7, which connects the B♭maj7 and Cm7 chords; in bar 3, beat 3, the A♭13 chord, bridging the A7♭13 and G7 chords. In bar 5 is a chromatic cliché—a Cm chord is embellished as the second-highest note descends in half steps to form a quick progression of Cm–Cm(maj7)–Cm7–Cm6. Throughout, there are chords with upper extensions—those notes beyond the seventh, like the #11 and ♭13—chords that add sophistication to this simple song.

Learning this arrangement might take you more than one week. It's important to practice it thoroughly until all the chords are under your fingers. And remember to think like a singer when playing this example and in the chord-melody style in general. You might be running through a handful of harmonies, but it's all about the melody.

✔ *BEGINNERS' TIP #4*

It's important to learn chord-melody arrangements by heart, in different keys and positions. This will improve not just your knowledge of the style but your fretboard fluency in general.

WEEK 4

Example 8

About the Authors

Ron Jackson

is a New York–based master jazz guitarist, composer, arranger, producer, and educator who's played with Taj Mahal, Jimmy McGriff, Randy Weston, Ron Carter, and others.
Select discography: *A Guitar Thing* (1991), *Akustik InventYours* (2014), *Standards and Other Songs* (2019)
practicejazzguitar.com

Adam Levy

is an itinerant guitarist based in Los Angeles. His work has appeared on recordings by Norah Jones, Lisa Loeb, Amos Lee, and Ani DiFranco, among others. He is also the founder of Guitar Tips Pro.
Select discography: *The Heart Collector* (2011), *Town & Country* (2014), *Blueberry Blonde* (2016)
guitartipspro.com

Sean McGowan

is a jazz guitarist based in Denver, where he directs the guitar program at the University of Colorado.
Select discography: *River Coffee* (2001), *Sphere: The Music of Thelonious Monk for Solo Guitar* (2011), *My Fair Lady* (2015)
seanmcgowanguitar.com

Jane Miller

is a guitar professor at Berklee College of music who has performed and presented master classes around the world. She is the author of *Introduction to Jazz Guitar* (Berklee Press/ Hal Leonard, 2015).
Select discography: *The Other Room* (2000), *Three Sides to a Story* (2013), *Boats* (2018)
janemillergroup.com

Jeffrey Pepper Rodgers

is a guitarist and singer-songwriter based in upstate New York. He is the founding editor of Acoustic Guitar magazine and current editor at large.
Select discography: *Humming My Way Back Home* (2007), *Stop, Drop, and Roll* (2010), *Almost There* (2014)
jeffreypepperrodgers.com

More Tools to Get You Started

Let the bestselling *Acoustic Guitar Method* by David Hamburger
be your guide to the joys of playing the guitar.

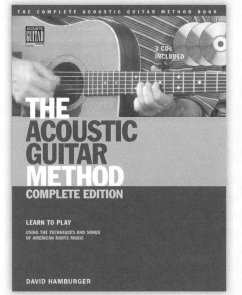

The COMPLETE Acoustic Guitar Method

The *Acoustic Guitar Method* is the only beginning guitar method based on traditional American music that teaches you authentic techniques and songs. From the folk and blues music of yesterday have come the rock, country, and jazz of today. Understand, play, and enjoy these essential traditions and styles on the instrument that truly represents American music, the acoustic guitar. This comprehensive approach is the one tool you need to get started.

$24.95, 136 pp., 9" x 12", HL00695667

Acoustic Guitar Method, Book One

LESSONS First Chords, First Song New Chord, New Strum Tab Basics and Your First Melody Reading Notes The G Chord The C Chord More Single Notes Country Backup Basics Seventh Chords Waltz Time Half Notes and Rests Minor Chords A Minor-Key Melody The B7 Chord.

SONGS Columbus Stockade Blues Careless Love Darling Corey East Virginia Blues In the Pines Banks of the Ohio Scarborough Fair Shady Grove Man of Constant Sorrow and more!

$9.95, 48 pp., 9" x 12", HL00695648

Acoustic Guitar Method, Book Two

LESSONS The Alternating Bass Blues in E Major Scales and Melodies Starting to Fingerpick More Picking Patterns The G-Major Scale Bass Runs More Bass Runs Blues Basics Alternating-Bass Fingerpicking Fingerpicking in 3/4.

SONGS Columbus Stockade Blues Stagolee The Girl I Left Behind Me Shady Grove Shenandoah Will the Circle Be Unbroken? Sail Away Ladies I Am a Pilgrim Bury Me Beneath the Willow Alberta Sugar Babe House of the Rising Sun.

$9.95, 48 pp., 9" x 12", HL00695649

Acoustic Guitar Method, Book Three

LESSONS The Swing Feel Tackling the F Chord More Chord Moves Introducing Travis Picking Travis Picking, Continued Hammer-ons, Slides, and Pull-offs Alternate Bass Notes The Pinch All Together Now.

SONGS Frankie and Johnny Delia Gambler's Blues Banks of the Ohio Crawdad New River Train Sail Away Ladies Little Sadie Omie Wise That'll Never Happen No More.

$9.95, 48 pp., 9" x 12", HL00695666

Dive Deeper into Chords, Slide, and Jazz

Learn authentic techniques and expand your understanding of musical essentials

The Acoustic Guitar Method Chord Book

David Hamburger's supplementary chord book for the *Acoustic Guitar Method* is a must-have resource for building your chord vocabulary! Start with a user-friendly explanation of what chords are and how they are named, then learn chords by key in all 12 keys, with both open-position and closed-position voicings for each common chord type.

$5.95, 48 pp., 9" x 12", HL00695722

Acoustic Guitar Slide Basics

Bitten by the blues bug? Want to explore the haunting sounds of acoustic slide guitar or brush up on your bottleneck basics? This easy-to-follow, step-by-step book and CD will help you master one of the great styles of American roots music. LESSONS Single-String Melodies Working in the Thumb Moving Around the Neck Spicing Up Your Melodies Travis Picking and more!

$16.95, 72 pp., 9" x 12", HL00695610

Early Jazz and Swing Songs for Guitar

Add early jazz and swing standards to your repertoire! Learn full guitar parts, read detailed notes on the song origins, and hear a two-guitar recording of each tune. SONGS After You've Gone Avalon Baby, Won't You Please Come Home Ballin' the Jack Hindustan Limehouse Blues Rose Room Saint James Infirmary St. Louis Blues Whispering and more! **$9.95**, 40 pp., 9" x 12", HL00695867

Buy online at
store.AcousticGuitar.com

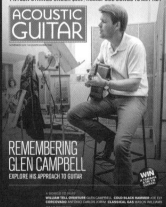